wok
bible

wok
bible

hamlyn

First published in Great Britain in 2003 by
Hamlyn, a division of Octopus Publishing Group Ltd
2–4 Heron Quays, London E14 4JP

Copyright © Octopus Publishing Group Ltd 2003

Produced for Borders USA in 2003 by
Hamlyn, a division of Octopus Publishing Group Ltd

ISBN 0 600 60990 1

A CIP catalogue record for this book is available from the British Library

Printed and bound in China

10 9 8 7 6 5 4 3 2 1

NOTES
Metric, imperial and American measurements have been given in all recipes.
Use one set of measurements only, and not a mixture.

This book includes dishes made with nuts and nut derivatives. It is advisable fo
people with known allergic reactions to nuts and nut derivatives and those wh
may be potentially vulnerable to these allergies, such as pregnant and nursing
mothers, invalids, the elderly, babies and children to avoid dishes made with
nuts and nut oils. It is also prudent to check the labels of pre-prepared
ingredients for the possible inclusion of nut derivatives.

Contents

Introduction 6

Light Bites 12

A Matter of Minutes 34

Stars of the East 56

Hale and Hearty 76

Spiced for Life 100

Notes for American readers

UK	US	UK	US
aubergine	eggplant	muscavado sugar	brown sugar
bicarbonate of soda	baking soda	natural yogurt	plain yogurt
caster sugar	superfine sugar	pak choi	bok choy
Chinese leaves	Napa cabbage	peppers	bell peppers
clingfilm	plastic wrap	plain flour	all-purpose flour
coriander	cilantro	pork fillet	pork tenderloin
cornflour	cornstarch	prawn crackers	shrimp chips
crystallized fruit	candied fruit	prawns	shrimp
dessiccated coconut	shredded coconut	rice vermicelli	rice noodles
		rump steak	round steak
double cream	heavy cream	self-raising flour	self-raising flour
filo pastry	phyllo pastry	soft brown sugar	brown sugar
full-fat milk	whole milk	soya	soy
groundnut oil	peanut oil	spring greens	collard greens
icing sugar	confectioner's sugar	spring onions	scallions
		sweetcorn	corn
jug	pitcher	tomato purée	tomato paste
mangetout	snow peas	vanilla essence	vanilla extract
minced pork	ground pork	wonton wrappers	wonton skins

Something Special   118

Sweet Temptations   140

Back to Basics   152

Index   158

Acknowledgements   160

Introduction

Woks are used all over South-east Asia. Usually made from thin carbon steel, their curved shape is designed for use over a fierce brazier. The rounded base fits neatly into a simple stand over an open flame, and the deep sides allow experienced cooks to shake and toss ingredients with skilful dexterity.

Woks have been used as the primary cooking utensil in the East for centuries, and have now become very popular in the West too. They are most commonly used for stir-frying, a quick and simple way to cook. Wok cookery is perfect for today's busy lifestyle, as most dishes are prepared very quickly and offer a wonderful opportunity to experiment with the wide range of exotic ingredients now available to us. However, a wok can also transform a few familiar, basic ingredients into a memorable meal.

Wok cooking is intrinsically healthy as the food is cooked only briefly, so the majority of nutrients are preserved. It is also healthy because in most dishes only a small amount of oil is used, no dairy products are involved and even red meat is trimmed of all fat before cooking. Most of the recipes in this book hail from Asia, from countries with such diverse culinary traditions as Malaysia, Indonesia, Vietnam, Thailand and China. Some feature special ingredients or unusual flavourings, which are described on pages 74–5 and 116–17.

Cooking in a wok

While stir-frying can be done successfully in a heavy-based frying pan, a wok is far better suited to the task. It is a large, metal pan with a rounded base and curved sides that allow the maximum spread of heat. Its depth ensures that the food can be stirred and tossed quickly without spilling. Because temperatures are so high, you need only a little oil to prevent sticking, and food can be pushed up the sides of the pan and out of the oil while it still cooks in the intense heat.

While woks are most commonly used for stir-frying, they are remarkably versatile and can also be used for other cooking methods, such as braising, steaming and deep-frying, making them a very useful all-purpose pan.

Woks can be used on both gas and electric hobs. A wok with a curved base may require a simple wire stand to support it, and flat-based woks are widely available. These are ideal for cooking on an electric hob.

Choosing a wok

Choose a large wok (about 35 cm/14 inches in diameter) with deep sides and a well-fitting lid, and check the material from which it is made or any coating on it before you buy. Some can be difficult to clean, while others can be put in a dishwasher. Woks may have one or two handles, which may be long or ear-shaped, and may be made from metal or wood. Wooden handles are safer.

Traditional Chinese wok
The Chinese wok, made of carbon steel, is the most popular type, even in the West. It is ideal for stir-frying as it conducts heat well and evenly, and heats up quickly. However, it needs to be seasoned (see page 8) and treated properly to prolong its life and prevent it from rusting. If food sticks to the sides and it has to be scrubbed, it will need to be seasoned again. Traditional steel woks are extremely practical if they are used frequently, but tend to rust if stored for long periods.

Nonstick wok
Nonstick woks are more expensive then traditional woks. They cannot be seasoned, which detracts slightly from the flavour of the food. They are not intended for use over fierce heat, which can be a disadvantage for rapid stir-frying. Many manufacturers recommend that they should not be preheated before adding oil. However, they

have the advantage of being easy to keep clean and quite practical. Buy suitable utensils to avoid scratching the nonstick surface.

Stainless steel
Stainless steel woks can be used over a high heat and stand up well to stir-frying. They are also good for braising and steaming. They often have a flattened base for use on electric or gas hobs. They are easily washable and should last for many years.

Wok accessories

Draining rack
This is a wire rack which fits around the inside edge of one side of the wok. Cooked food can be placed on it to drain back into the pan and to stay hot while cooking other ingredients. They are useful when you are deep-frying in batches.

Lid
A dome-shaped lid is essential if you want to use the wok for steaming. You could use an ordinary pan lid, if it fits the wok, or as a last resort, cover it with foil.

Stand
A metal ring designed to keep a round-based wok steady on the hob.

Steaming rack
A small round grid or trivet that can be placed in the base of the wok over a small quantity of water for steaming.

Bamboo steamer
These baskets can be stacked in a wok and have a lid of their own. The larger ones are most practical and allow space for more water underneath them. Most steamer sets come with two layers, but you can use more.

Ladle
A shallow ladle is often used in wok cookery for adding liquid to the ingredients. It is also used for scooping out cooked food. Stainless steel is the most suitable material, as wooden or plastic ladles are easily scorched.

Wooden spatula or spoon
Use this for tossing and turning ingredients in the wok and for serving cooked food.

Chopsticks
These are also good for stirring and for lifting foods in and out of the wok. Special long chopsticks are used for cooking.

Slotted spoon or skimmer
Use one of these for lifting cooked foods out of the wok. They are especially good for fried foods, as they allow oil to drain away.

Frying baskets
Use a large one for deep-frying small items. Place the food in the basket, lower it into hot oil and leave it there until the food is cooked, when it can be lifted out and drained.

Wire baskets

Small wire baskets on bamboo handles are useful for lifting food in and out of hot oil when deep-frying or from stock when braising. Like a frying basket, they allow the oil or liquid to drain away as the item is lifted.

Bamboo brush

A bundle of stiff, split bamboo, used for cleaning. This is the traditional way to clean a wok without abrasive scouring, using hot water (see 'Seasoning', right).

Chopping boards

Chopping is one of the most important parts of most wok recipes, so it is worth making sure that you have chopping boards that are adequate for your needs. Use separate boards for raw and cooked ingredients. Solid wood is the most popular choice, but rigid polythene is ideal for poultry as it can be sterilized and is dishwasher-safe.

Sharp knives

A selection of good-quality kitchen knives for slicing and chopping fresh ingredients, including meat, fish and vegetables, will make the job safer and more enjoyable – and you'll get better results and neater pieces. Use a thin-bladed knife for fine shredding and vegetable preparation and a heavier knife for cutting up meat. You may also need a large, heavy knife or cleaver for chopping through bones.

Knife sharpener

Sharp knives are easier to use and safer than blunt ones.

Food processor

This can be useful for making spice and curry pastes using garlic, ginger and other herbs and spices. They are also useful if you prefer to mince meat yourself, rather than buy it ready prepared.

Pestle and mortar

This traditional tool is used for grinding seeds and spices or pounding pastes. Ceramic mortars usually have an unglazed inner surface that is slightly abrasive. Pestles and mortars may also be made of metal or wood, although the latter are less practical and versatile.

Seasoning a wok

All new woks, other than nonstick ones, will have been coated by the manufacturer with an oil or wax film to prevent them from rusting. You need to remove this film to prepare the wok for use and then season it to ensure that you get many years of service from it.

● Start by heating the wok over a very high heat until it is extremely hot. Allow it to cool enough to handle it, then scrub it in warm, soapy water using a scourer or brush. Put it back over the heat to dry.

● Using a piece of kitchen paper, rub the surface of the wok with vegetable oil, then heat the wok until the oil smokes. This will prevent it from rusting and create a nonstick surface. Leave the wok to cool, then wipe off any excess oil before putting it away ready for use.

● After use, rinse the wok in hot water, without detergent, using a stiff brush to get off any pieces of food. Dry thoroughly, then wipe the inside with an oil-soaked piece of kitchen paper. Repeat this each time you use your wok and it will build up a smooth, shiny, nonstick surface.

● If the wok becomes rusty through infrequent use, scrub and season it again.

Cooking methods

The most common methods of wok cooking are stir-frying, steaming, braising and deep-frying. The following techniques are easy to master and allow you to try different recipes from all over Asia.

Stir-frying

This entails simply frying foods in a small amount of oil over a high heat, stirring constantly. It ensures that the food is sealed and cooked very quickly, retaining its flavour, texture and colour – all of which are vitally important to the success of the finished dish. The curved shape and large surface area of a wok assists the drainage of oil and allows plenty of room for the food to be tossed and turned while it is cooked.

The key to successful stir-frying is to have all the ingredients measured out and chopped or sliced before you heat the wok, as the cooking takes only a few minutes. When cooking a variety of ingredients together, add them in stages, starting with those that require the longest cooking. Stir-fried foods should not be overcooked or greasy. For more stir-fry hints and tips, see pages 32–3.

Deep-frying

A wok is practical for deep-frying relatively small quantities of food, but it is not sufficiently stable for cooking with a lot of oil. Use a fairly shallow depth of oil, never more than half-filling the wok, as the level will rise when it is heated and the food added. It is often best to cook ingredients in small batches. Always ensure that ingredients are thoroughly dry before adding them to hot oil, to prevent it from spitting.

Steaming

Steaming is a very healthy way to prepare food and helps to retain the flavour, texture and colour of the ingredients. The food is placed on a rack or trivet over a little boiling water or stock and cooked gently in the steam. This is ideal for foil-wrapped parcels. Ingredients may also be steamed in a shallow dish or on a plate. Alternatively, a bamboo steamer can be placed inside the wok resting against and supported by the sides above the water level.

To prevent ingredients from sticking, line the steamer with cabbage or banana leaves or with greaseproof paper. A average wok holds enough water for short periods of steaming; check the level during cooking and top up with more boiling water if necessary. Steaming is particularly well suited to foods with a delicate flavour or texture, such as fish and vegetables.

Boiling

Unless you intend to season it thoroughly with oil, a traditional carbon steel wok is not ideal for boiling. Small quantities of noodles can be softened in simmering water, but a saucepan is more practical for boiling a large portion, or for items that require longer cooking.

Soups can also be prepared in a wok – an average-sized wok should have ample space for four regular portions or six modest servings.

Stir-braising

This is often a stage that follows on from stir-frying, when liquid is added to the stir-fried ingredients. The ingredients are simmered gently for a short period and stirred frequently during cooking.

Red braising

This Chinese method of cooking entails braising food in a mixture of soy sauce, water and sugar with additional flavourings, such as ginger, spring onion and rice wine. The food takes on a red tinge during the cooking process. It is best suited to tougher cuts of meat or vegetables, which take some time to cook.

Authentic ingredients

Authentic wok cookery is not possible without the use of certain ingredients, spices and sauces that add a distinctive flavour and colour. These are widely available from Oriental food stores. As so many Chinese people now live abroad, many major cities have their own Chinatown area, with colourful shops, restaurants and food stores. Just browsing around gives an excellent insight into the rich diversity of both culture and cuisine, and many of these shops stock ingredients from other Asian countries, including Thailand and Vietnam.

Another excellent source of Asian ingredients is your nearest large supermarket. Wok cookery has become so popular that many of the basic ingredients are readily available there. See pages 74–5 and 116–7 for details of some of the typical ingredients you may need.

Rice

There are many different types of rice, including long-grain, short-grain and glutinous varieties. Brown rice is not used in South-east Asian cookery as most people dislike its texture. The most popular type is long-grain white rice. In Thai cookery, fragrant rice is also widely used; it is always cooked without adding salt to the pan. Glutinous or sticky rice is a medium-grain rice that becomes sweet and sticky when cooked. It is used for baked and sweet dishes. The name is something of a misnomer as it does not contain gluten.

Oil

Oil is commonly used as a cooking medium in wok cookery. Groundnut oil is a good choice as it is mild, making it excellent for stir-frying and deep-frying. Safflower and sunflower oils are also good choices.

Sesame oil is also frequently used in wok cookery, especially in Chinese dishes. However, it is usually used as a flavouring rather than as a cooking oil, as it burns easily and the flavour is strong. It is usually added at the last minute to season and finish a dish.

Garnishes

Frequently used in Chinese and Thai recipes, Oriental garnishes add an authentic touch to any Asian dish and they are easier to make than they look.

A wide range of pretty garnishes can be used to decorate the recipes in this book, from sprigs of herbs like coriander and mint to ornate spring onion tassels and chilli flowers. Cucumber and lemon slices will also add a fresh splash of colour to dishes.

Chilli flowers

Cut a fresh red chilli lengthways into four quarters, from the tip almost to the base, leaving the stalk intact. Use the point of a sharp knife to scrape out the seeds. Make lengthways cuts in the flesh, keeping the stalk end attached, then drop it into a bowl of iced water and chill in the refrigerator for at least 30 minutes. The chilli will then open out like a flower. Drain well before using.

Spring onion tassels

Remove and discard the root end from a spring onion and trim the stem to about 7.5 cm (3 inches) long. Cut lengthways through the green end of the onion, leaving the white end intact. Turn the onion round slightly and cut again; repeat once or twice more to shred the end of the onion into a tassel. As with the chilli flowers, put the onion in a bowl of iced water and chill in the refrigerator for about an hour, until the tassel ends curl.

Tomato rose

You will need a firm tomato to make this garnish. Use a sharp knife to remove the skin in one continuous spiral strip, starting at the smooth end. Make the strip about 1 cm (½ inch) wide. With the skin side out, start to wind up the strip from the base end to form a bud shape. Continue winding until you have a rose.

Radish roses

Remove the stalk from a radish and use a small sharp knife to cut a series of petal-shapes in a row around the bottom, leaving them attached at their bases. Cut a second row of petal shapes above the first row. Continue cutting rows of petals until you

reach the top of the radish. Drop the radish into iced water and chill in the refrigerator for several hours, until the petals open out.

Cucumber and lemon slices

Cucumber and lemon or lime slices make an attractive garnish and can be used flat, or curled and standing up. Use the notch on a canelle knife or a sharp paring knife to remove strips of peel lengthways down a cucumber or lemon, then slice into thin rings. To make curls, cut the slice from one edge to the centre, then twist the two cut edges apart and stand the slice on them.

chapter 1

Light Bites

Delicious finger food for parties,
Oriental-style appetizers and starters,
and light snacks for all occasions.
This chapter also features hints
and tips to help you make the most
of your wok and perfect your
stir-frying skills.

Cellophane Noodle Soup

Preparation time: 10 minutes
Cooking time: 10 minutes

Serves 4

2 tablespoons vegetable oil
2 teaspoons Garlic Mixture (see page 155)
250 g (8 oz) minced pork
1 litre (1¾ pints, 4½ cups) Chicken Stock (see
    page 154)
125 g (4 oz) cellophane noodles
4 spring onions, cut into 2.5 cm (1 inch) lengths
½ onion, finely chopped
2 tablespoons Thai fish sauce
2 teaspoons salt
250 g (8 oz) raw tiger prawns, peeled and deveined
2 celery sticks with leaves, sliced
pepper

1 Heat the oil in a wok, add the garlic mixture and stir-fry for 1 minute.

2 Add the minced pork and stir-fry for 3 minutes, then pour in the stock and bring to the boil. Stir in the noodles, spring onions, onion, fish sauce and salt. Bring the soup back to the boil and cook for 3 minutes. Lower the heat, add the prawns and celery and simmer for a further 2 minutes.

3 Transfer to a warm serving bowl, season with pepper and serve immediately.

wok tip
To prepare the prawns, pull off the heads and peel off the shells. Slit each prawn along the length of its back with a knife, then remove the dark digestive cord inside with the tip of the knife and discard.

Spring Rolls

Preparation time: 20 minutes
Cooking time: 40 minutes

Serves 6

250 g (8 oz) 12 cm (5 inch) square spring roll
    wrappers
1 egg, beaten
oil, for deep-frying

FILLING:
2 tablespoons vegetable oil
2 tablespoons Garlic Mixture (see page 155)
125 g (4 oz, ½ cup) drained canned or thawed
    frozen crabmeat
125 g (4 oz) raw tiger prawns, peeled, deveined and
    finely chopped
125 g (4 oz) minced pork
125 g (4 oz) dried rice vermicelli, soaked and cut into
    1 cm (½ inch) lengths
125 g (4 oz, 1½ cups) mushrooms, finely chopped
2 tablespoons Thai fish sauce
2 tablespoons light soy sauce
1 teaspoon sugar
5 spring onions, finely chopped

TO GARNISH:
1 large fresh red chilli, deseeded and cut into thin
    strips
1 lime, sliced
fresh basil leaves

1 To make the filling, heat the oil in a wok, add the garlic mixture and stir-fry for 1 minute, until golden brown. Add the crabmeat, prawns and pork and stir-fry for 10–12 minutes. Add the rice vermicelli, mushrooms, fish sauce, soy sauce, sugar and spring onions and stir-fry for a further 5 minutes until all the liquid has been absorbed. Set aside to cool.

2 Separate the spring roll wrappers and spread them out under a clean tea towel to keep them soft. Put about 2 tablespoons of the filling on each wrapper, and brush the left and right borders with beaten egg.

3 Fold the sides over the filling and then roll up to a sausage shape. Brush the top edge with more beaten egg and then seal. Keep the filled rolls covered while you make the remaining rolls in the same way.

4 Heat the oil in a wok and cook the rolls, a few at a time, for 5–8 minutes, or until golden brown. Turn once during cooking so that they brown evenly. Drain on kitchen paper and serve hot, garnished with strips of red chilli, slices of lime and a few basil leaves.

Fried Wontons

Preparation time: 15 minutes
Cooking time: 20 minutes

Serves 4–5

250 g (8 oz) minced pork
1 tablespoon finely chopped onion
2 teaspoons Garlic Mixture (see page 155)
2 tablespoons Thai fish sauce
20 Wonton Wrappers (see page 157)
1 egg yolk, beaten
oil, for deep-frying
1 spring onion, thinly sliced, to garnish
Chilli Sauce (see page 156) or plum sauce, to serve

1 Put the minced pork in a small bowl with the chopped onion, garlic mixture and fish sauce. Mix thoroughly to combine all the ingredients to a thick paste.

2 Spread out the wonton wrappers on a work surface and put a teaspoon of the pork mixture into the centre of each wrapper.

3 Brush the edges of the wrappers with the egg yolk and then fold the wrappers over, gathering the edges together and completely enclosing the filling. Seal the tops with more egg yolk if necessary.

4 Heat the oil in a wok and fry the filled wontons, a few at a time, for about 5 minutes, until they are golden brown. Turn them over in the oil if necessary to brown both sides. Drain on kitchen paper, garnish with slices of spring onion and serve hot with chilli sauce or plum sauce or both if you prefer.

wok tip
You can make your own wonton wrappers (see page 157), or buy them ready prepared from Chinese supermarkets. Wontons can also be simmered in soup for a filling lunch or starter.

Crispy Seaweed

Preparation time: 5 minutes, plus drying
Cooking time: 10 minutes

Serves 8

750 g (1½ lb) spring greens
vegetable oil, for deep-frying
1½ teaspoons caster sugar
1 teaspoon salt

1 Separate the leaves of the spring greens. Wash them well and then pat dry with kitchen paper or a clean tea towel.

2 Using a very sharp knife, shred the spring greens into the thinnest possible shavings. Spread out the shreds on kitchen paper and leave for about 30 minutes, until they are thoroughly dry.

3 In a wok, heat the oil to 180–190°C (350–375°F), or until a cube of bread browns in 30 seconds. Turn off the heat for 30 seconds, then add a small batch of spring green shreds. Turn on the heat to moderate and deep-fry the greens until they begin to float. Take care as they tend to spit while they are cooking.

4 Remove the greens with a slotted spoon and drain them on kitchen paper. Cook the remaining greens in batches in the same way. When they are all cooked, transfer to a bowl and sprinkle with the sugar and salt. Toss gently to mix and serve warm or cold.

wok tip
Don't overcrowd the wok when deep-frying. This will lower the temperature of the oil and the greens will not become crisp.

Vegetable Pakoras

Preparation time: 25 minutes
Cooking time: 15 minutes

Serves 4–6

125 g (4 oz, 1 cup) chickpea flour
about 275 ml (9 fl oz, 1 cup plus 2 tablespoons)
   water
½ teaspoon ground turmeric
½ teaspoon ground cumin
½ teaspoon paprika
½ teaspoon bicarbonate of soda
vegetable oil, for deep-frying
500 g (1 lb) assorted vegetables: cauliflower florets,
   sweet potato slices, thickly sliced onion, segments
   of red and green peppers, baby aubergines and
   slices of aubergine

CORIANDER RELISH:
25 g (1 oz, 1 cup) fresh coriander leaves, chopped
2 fresh green chillies, deseeded and finely chopped
4 tablespoons water
1 tablespoon lemon juice
300 ml (½ pint, 1¼ cups) natural yogurt
2 teaspoons ground cumin
2 teaspoons caster sugar

1 First make the relish. Process the coriander leaves and green chillies with the water and lemon juice in a food processor. Stir into the yogurt with the ground cumin and sugar. Cover and chill until required.

2 Mix the chickpea flour with enough water to make a smooth and thick batter that will cling to the vegetables. Add the turmeric, cumin, paprika and bicarbonate of soda and mix together.

3 Heat the oil in a wok until a cube of bread browns in 1 minute. Dip a few vegetables into the batter, then put them straight into the hot oil and deep-fry for 1–2 minutes, depending on their thickness. Remove from the oil and drain on kitchen paper, then repeat with the remaining vegetables. Serve the pakoras with the coriander relish, while still crisp and warm.

wok tip
Pakoras are a great Indian finger food, and the Coriander Relish makes the perfect accompaniment. All manner of vegetables can be covered in the batter and deep-fried, so use whatever you have.

Vietnamese Chicken Rolls

1 To make the filling, drain the cellophane noodles, then cut them into 2.5 cm (1 inch) pieces. Drain and finely chop the mushrooms, discarding any tough stems.

2 Combine the noodles, mushrooms, chicken, garlic, shallots, crabmeat and pepper in a bowl, mixing well. Divide the mixture into 20 portions and shape each into a small cylinder.

3 To assemble a chicken roll, brush beaten egg over the entire surface of a rice paper wrapper. Leave the wrapper for a few seconds until it is soft and flexible. Place a portion of the filling near the curved edge of the wrapper and roll both filling and wrapper once. Then fold over the sides of the wrapper to enclose the filling and continue rolling. The beaten egg holds the wrapper together. Repeat with the remaining rice paper wrappers and filling.

4 Heat the oil in a wok to 180–190°C (350–375°F), or until a cube of bread browns in 30 seconds, and deep-fry about one-third of the chicken rolls over a moderate heat until golden brown. Remove the rolls from the oil with a slotted spoon and set aside to drain on kitchen paper. Fry the remaining chicken rolls in the same way. Serve hot or at room temperature with tangy chilli sauce.

Preparation time: 30 minutes, plus soaking
Cooking time: 20 minutes

Serves 4–6

4 eggs, beaten
20 rice paper spring roll wrappers
vegetable oil, for deep-frying
Chilli Sauce (see page 156), to serve

FILLING:
50 g (2 oz) cellophane noodles, soaked in water for 10 minutes
2 dried shiitake mushrooms, soaked in hot water for 30 minutes
500 g (1 lb) boneless, skinless chicken breast, cut into thin strips
3 garlic cloves, finely chopped
3 shallots, finely chopped
250 g (8 oz) drained canned or thawed frozen crabmeat
1/2 teaspoon pepper

wok tip
Cooked chicken rolls can be frozen, then reheated in the oven. Alternatively, they can be partially cooked, stored in the refrigerator for up to 1 day and the cooking completed before serving.

20   light bites

Green Peppers Stuffed with Pork and Ginger

Preparation time: 15 minutes
Cooking time: 30–35 minutes

Serves 4–6

1 tablespoon sunflower oil
1 garlic clove, crushed
2.5 cm (1 inch) piece fresh root ginger, peeled and finely chopped
250 g (8 oz) lean minced pork
1 spring onion, chopped
1 celery stick, finely chopped
grated rind of 1 lemon
4 green peppers

1 Heat the oil in a wok over a moderate heat. Add the garlic and stir-fry until lightly browned. Reduce the heat, add the ginger and pork and stir-fry for 2 minutes.

2 Add the spring onion, celery and lemon rind. Combine well and stir-fry for another 30 seconds. Let the mixture cool slightly.

3 Cut the peppers into quarters and remove the core and seeds. Divide the mixture between the 16 quarters, pressing it down into each of the cavities.

4 Arrange the pepper quarters in an oiled, ovenproof dish. Cook in a preheated oven, 200°C (400°F), Gas Mark 6, for 25 minutes, until tender.

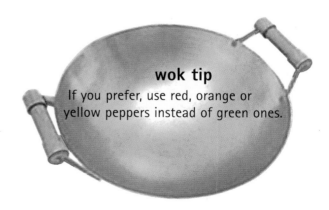

wok tip
If you prefer, use red, orange or yellow peppers instead of green ones.

Crab Cakes

Preparation time: 15 minutes, plus chilling
Cooking time: 20 minutes

Serves 4

wok tip
Try to use fresh crabmeat for this dish – frozen crabmeat is always very wet and quite often fairly tasteless.

450 g (14½ oz) mixed white and brown crabmeat
2 small shallots, finely chopped
1 garlic clove, finely chopped
1 tablespoon chopped fresh coriander
1 tablespoon Thai fish sauce
½ teaspoon pepper
½ egg, beaten
breadcrumbs (optional)
vegetable oil, for frying
chive flowers, to garnish
Soy and Vinegar Dipping Sauce (see page 156), to serve

1 Put the crabmeat, shallots, garlic, coriander, fish sauce, pepper and egg into a bowl and mix together, then form into 12–16 cakes. If the crabmeat was frozen and the mixture is too sloppy, add some breadcrumbs to thicken. Place the cakes on a plate and chill in the refrigerator for about 1 hour to firm up.

2 Heat about 5 mm (¼ inch) of oil in a wok and add 4 crab cakes. Cook, without stirring or turning, for 2–3 minutes, until brown and crusty underneath. Turn them over carefully and cook for a further 2–3 minutes, then remove and drain on kitchen paper. Cook the remainder in the same way. Garnish the crab cakes with chive flowers and serve with the dipping sauce.

Prawns with Broccoli

Preparation time: 10 minutes, plus marinating
Cooking time: 5 minutes

Serves 2–3

250 g (8 oz) cooked king prawns, peeled and deveined
1 slice fresh root ginger, peeled and finely chopped
1 tablespoon rice wine or dry sherry
1 egg white
1 teaspoon cornflour
3 tablespoons vegetable oil
2 spring onions, finely chopped
250 g (8 oz) broccoli, cut into florets
1 teaspoon salt
½ teaspoon sugar

1 Wash the prawns, and dry them thoroughly on kitchen paper. Split each prawn in half lengthways and then cut it into pieces.

2 Put the prawn pieces in a small bowl with the ginger, rice wine or sherry, egg white and cornflour. Stir well and leave in a cool place or in the refrigerator to marinate for about 20 minutes.

3 Heat 1 tablespoon of the oil in a wok and add the prawn mixture. Stir-fry over a moderate heat for about 30 seconds. Remove from the wok with a slotted spoon.

4 Heat the remaining oil in the wok. Add the spring onions and broccoli and stir well. Add the salt and sugar, then stir-fry until the broccoli is just tender. Stir in the cooked prawns and serve hot.

wok tip
Small cooked prawns work just as well in this recipe. Buy them with the shells on and peel them yourself for the best flavour.

Potato and Fenugreek Samosas

Preparation time: 30 minutes, plus cooling
Cooking time: 1 hour

Serves 6

175 g (6 oz, 1½ cups) plain flour
75 g (3 oz, ⅓ cup) butter
about 4 tablespoons cold water
vegetable oil, for deep-frying
mango chutney, to serve

FILLING:
6 tablespoons vegetable oil
1 large onion, finely chopped
1 fresh green chilli, deseeded and finely chopped
2 teaspoons ground turmeric
2 teaspoons ground cumin
2 teaspoons ground coriander
2.5 cm (1 inch) piece of fresh root ginger, peeled and grated
2 tablespoons dried fenugreek
375 g (12 oz, 2½ cups) potatoes, finely diced

wok tip
Samosas are great snacks and perfect picnic food. To enjoy them at their crunchy best, eat them the day you make them.

1 To make the pastry, place the flour in a bowl, add the butter and rub in with the fingertips until it resembles fine breadcrumbs. Add the water, 1 tablespoon at a time, until a soft but firm dough forms. Knead lightly for 5 minutes, then wrap in clingfilm and chill for 1 hour.

2 Meanwhile, heat the vegetable oil, add the onion and cook until soft and beginning to brown. Add the green chilli, turmeric, cumin, coriander and ginger and stir-fry for 2–3 minutes. Add the fenugreek and diced potatoes and continue to cook for a further 8–10 minutes, stirring frequently. Remove from the heat and leave to cool.

3 Knead the samosa pastry once more and divide into 12 walnut-size balls. Keeping the remaining balls covered with a tea towel, flatten 1 ball and roll out to a 15 cm (6 inch) circle. Cut the circle in half and form each semi-circle into a cone shape, sealing the edge with water. Fill the cavity with 2 teaspoons of the potato mixture and turn the top side over, again sealing with water. Repeat with the remaining pastry and filling.

4 Heat the oil for deep-frying in a wok until a cube of bread browns in 1 minute. Slide 2 samosas into the oil and cook for 2 minutes on one side, then turn them over and cook until the second side is golden brown. Remove with a slotted spoon and drain on kitchen paper. Deep-fry the remaining samosas in the same way and serve warm with mango chutney.

Spicy Chicken Satay

Preparation time: 20 minutes, plus marinating
Cooking time: 30–35 minutes

Serves 4

8 chicken wings
1 tablespoon ground almonds
1 tablespoon ground ginger
1 teaspoon ground coriander
pinch of chilli powder
1 teaspoon ground turmeric
300 ml (½ pint, 1¼ cups) Coconut Milk (see page 156)
1 small red pepper, deseeded and finely chopped
1 teaspoon palm sugar or light brown sugar
salt and pepper

SATAY SAUCE:
2 onions, coarsely chopped
200 g (7 oz, 1⅓ cups) peanuts, roasted
pinch of chilli powder
2 tablespoons oil
125 ml (4 fl oz, ½ cup) water
1 teaspoon sugar
1 tablespoon soy sauce
2 tablespoons lemon juice

wok tip
Roasting the peanuts gives the sauce a much more intense nutty flavour. Heat a wok until hot, then dry-fry the nuts, stirring constantly, until they turn golden. Remove from the wok and allow to cool.

TO GARNISH:
chopped fresh coriander
bay leaves (optional)

TO SERVE:
lemon wedges
1 red and 1 yellow pepper, cored, deseeded and finely diced

1 Sprinkle the chicken with salt and pepper and place in a shallow dish. To make the marinade, mix together the ground almonds, ginger, coriander, chilli and turmeric in a bowl, then gradually add the coconut milk. Stir in the red pepper, then pour the mixture over the chicken and leave to marinate for about 2 hours.

2 Meanwhile, make the satay sauce. Place half of the chopped onions in a blender or food processor, add the peanuts and chilli powder and process to a paste. Heat the oil in a wok, add the remaining onion, and sauté until soft. Add the peanut paste and cook, stirring, for 3 minutes. Gradually add the measured water, stirring constantly. Stir in the sugar and cook for 5 minutes. Stir in the soy sauce and lemon juice. Keep hot.

3 Drain the chicken and reserve the marinade. Sprinkle with the brown sugar and cook under a preheated hot grill for 15–20 minutes, until the chicken is cooked and crisp. Turn the wings frequently and baste with the marinade. Serve the wings with the lemon wedges, diced peppers and, in a separate small bowl, the satay sauce. Garnish with chopped coriander and bay leaves, if using.

Stuffed Thai Omelette

Preparation time: 10 minutes
Cooking time: 12–17 minutes

Serves 2

3 tablespoons vegetable oil
1 garlic clove, crushed
125 g (4 oz) minced pork
1 tablespoon Thai fish sauce
½ teaspoon sugar
125 g (4 oz, ⅔ cup) onion, finely chopped
1 tomato, skinned and chopped
3 eggs, beaten
pepper

TO GARNISH:
fresh coriander sprigs
2 red chilli flowers (see page 10)

1 Heat 2 tablespoons of the oil in a wok. Add the garlic and stir-fry quickly until just golden. Add the minced pork, fish sauce, sugar, onion and tomato, and season with pepper.

2 Stir-fry the pork and vegetable mixture for 5–10 minutes, until the pork is lightly browned and the onion is golden, but not brown. Set aside and keep warm.

3 Heat the remaining oil in a clean wok, tilting it so that the oil coats the entire surface. Pour away and discard any excess oil. Add the beaten eggs, tilting the wok to form an omelette.

4 Put the stir-fried vegetable and pork mixture in the centre of the cooked omelette. Fold down the four sides, like a parcel. Serve immediately, folded-side down, garnished with coriander sprigs and chilli flowers.

wok tip
To remove the skin from the tomato, place it in a bowl of boiling water for 1 minute. The skin should simply peel away. If it does not, return it to the water for another minute.

Northern Thai Salad

Preparation time: 20 minutes, plus soaking
Cooking time: 5–10 minutes

Serves 4

250 g (8 oz) cellophane noodles
2 tablespoons vegetable oil
175 g (6 oz) minced pork
4 garlic cloves, crushed
1 teaspoon sugar
125 g (4 oz) cooked, peeled prawns
2 shallots, thinly sliced
2 tablespoons Thai fish sauce
1 tablespoon lime juice
1 teaspoon caster sugar
2 small fresh red chillies, deseeded and finely chopped
2 small fresh green chillies, deseeded and finely chopped
3 tablespoons Crushed Roasted Peanuts (see page 157), plus extra to serve
2 tablespoons chopped fresh coriander leaves

TO GARNISH:
2 spring onions, diagonally sliced
1 large fresh red chilli, deseeded and diagonally sliced
fresh coriander sprigs

1 Soak the noodles in warm water for about 20 minutes. Rinse in cold water, drain well and, using a pair of scissors, snip them into shorter lengths.

2 Heat the oil in a wok and fry the pork until cooked through. Add the garlic and sugar and stir-fry for 3 minutes.

3 Remove from the heat and stir the pork mixture into the noodles. Add the prawns, shallots, fish sauce, lime juice, sugar, chillies, peanuts and coriander. Toss the ingredients together and serve in heaped portions, garnished with spring onions, red chilli and coriander sprigs. Serve with extra crushed roasted peanuts.

wok tip
This crunchy, cold noodle salad has plenty of tang and fiery chilli. In parts of Thailand, it is served with pickled garlic cloves and a delicious local sausage, which is similar to the Spanish chorizo.

Artichokes with Red Peppers

Preparation time: 20 minutes, plus cooling
Cooking time: about 5 minutes

Serves 4

1 large red pepper
2 tablespoons vegetable oil
1 onion, finely chopped
2.5 cm (1 inch) piece of fresh root ginger, peeled and
    finely chopped
1 garlic clove, crushed
300 g (10 oz) can artichoke hearts, drained and sliced
1 tablespoon balsamic vinegar
salt and pepper
fresh basil leaves, to garnish

wok tip
Roasted red pepper is soft
and sweet, with a smoky flavour.
If you are short of time, you can
omit roasting the red pepper, but
you will need to stir-fry it for a
few minutes longer to soften it.

1 Roast the red pepper under a hot grill, turning it frequently, until the skin is charred on all sides. Wrap it in kitchen paper, place immediately in a plastic bag and close tightly. Leave until cool enough to handle.

2 Unwrap the red pepper and rub off the blackened skin under cold running water. Pull out and discard the core and seeds, then cut the pepper open lengthways, rinse and pat dry with kitchen paper. Cut the pepper lengthways into thin strips, then set aside.

3 Heat the oil in a wok over a moderate heat. Add the onion, ginger and garlic and stir-fry for 2–3 minutes, or until softened, but not browned. Add the artichoke hearts and pepper strips, increase the heat to high and toss until piping hot. Sprinkle over the balsamic vinegar and add salt and pepper to taste. Serve immediately, garnished with basil leaves.

Crispy Rice with Dipping Sauce

Preparation time: 15 minutes, plus drying
Cooking time: 25 minutes

Serves 4

250 g (8 oz, 1¼ cups) glutinous rice
vegetable oil, for deep-frying

DIPPING SAUCE:
125 ml (4 fl oz, ½ cup) Coconut Milk (see page 156)
50 g (2 oz) minced pork
50 g (2 oz) cooked peeled prawns, finely chopped
1 teaspoon Garlic Mixture (see page 155)
1½ tablespoons Thai fish sauce
1½ tablespoons sugar
50 g (2 oz, ⅓ cup) onion, finely chopped
50 g (2 oz, ⅓ cup) Crushed Roasted Peanuts
   (see page 157)

1 Place the rice in a saucepan and pour in enough water to cover. Bring to the boil, cover and cook until the rice is thoroughly cooked and sticky. Drain the rice in a sieve. Spread the rice out in a thin layer on greased baking trays, pressing down well. Set aside to dry in a warm place or in a preheated oven, 120°C (250°F), Gas Mark ½.

2 Meanwhile, make the dipping sauce. Pour the coconut milk into a wok and gradually bring to the boil. Add the minced pork and prawns, stirring to break up any lumps. Stir in the garlic mixture, fish sauce, sugar, onion and roasted peanuts. Reduce the heat and simmer the sauce for 20 minutes, stirring occasionally.

3 When completely dry and firm, remove the rice from the trays with a spatula, breaking it into large flat pieces.

4 Heat the oil for deep-frying in a wok to 180–190°C (350–375°F), or until a cube of bread browns in 30 seconds. Deep-fry the rice pieces until golden. You should hear the grains beginning to pop after about 5 seconds. Remove from the oil with a slotted spoon and drain on kitchen paper. Serve the crispy rice pieces with the dipping sauce.

wok tip
When boiling rice, Thai cooks reserve the layer of sticky grain left in the bottom of the saucepan to make this dish, mixing it with the drained rice before leaving it to dry.

Stir-fry hints and tips

Preparation

● Prepare and chop or slice all fresh ingredients in advance so that they are ready to be added to the wok when required. You won't have time to prepare anything while you are cooking.

● Cut each type of meat and vegetable into similar-size pieces so that all the pieces cook at the same speed and are ready at the same time. This also improves the presentation of the finished dish.

● Cut ingredients into relatively small pieces so that they cook right through to the centre without overcooking the outside. It also makes eating with chopsticks easier if the pieces are bite sized.

● Measure out sauces, flavourings and dry ingredients before you begin cooking. Divide them into separate bowls of those which are added at the same time.

● Use a good-quality light oil for stir-frying, such as groundnut, safflower or sunflower.

● Cut spring onions into diagonal slices or chunks as these are far more attractive than round slices.

● Fresh root ginger and galangal can be sliced, finely chopped or grated, depending on the texture of the finished dish.

Cooking

● For best results, preheat the wok over a moderate heat before adding the oil, then heat it again with the oil. The oil should be extremely hot, but not smoking, so that the pan retains as much heat as possible once you start cooking. Add the first ingredients and keep the heat high so the food seals on the outside and cooks quickly.

● Use two hands while stir-frying – one to hold the handle of the wok and the other to move the food around with chopsticks or a spatula. Keep the food moving all the time to prevent it from sticking and ensure that it cooks evenly.

● Add the ingredients which will take longest to cook to the wok first, gradually moving on to those which cook quickest. This should ensure that all the ingredients are cooked to perfection at exactly the same moment.

10 golden rules for stir-frying

1 Use a large wok and an intense heat source.

2 Prepare, measure and chop or slice all the ingredients before you begin.

3 Cut food into similar-sized pieces so that it all cooks evenly.

4 Preheat the wok before adding the oil.

5 Heat the oil until it is almost smoking before you add the first ingredients.

6 Put the slowest cooking ingredients into the wok first, gradually moving on to the those which cook quickest.

7 Keep stirring and tossing the food while cooking.

8 Keep the heat high so that the food cooks quickly.

9 Do not allow food to start boiling in its own juices – turn the heat up if it looks wet.

10 Never overcook stir-fried food.

Carefully follow the order of ingredients in the recipes in this book; they are designed so that everything is cooked through by the end of the cooking time.

● Do not allow the food to start boiling in its own juices, especially fresh meat and vegetables. If any liquid does ooze out of the ingredients, turn up the heat to evaporate it as quickly as possible – you should be frying the food, not boiling it.

● Never overcook stir-fried food. Meat should be tender and just cooked through, while vegetables should still be crisp and fresh and retain their vivid colour. Serve the dish immediately it is cooked. It will continue to cook after you've turned the heat off and may become overcooked and soggy if you leave it too long before eating.

chapter 2
A Matter of Minutes

None of these recipes take more than 30 minutes – and most can be put together much more quickly. There are mouthwatering fish, meat and vegetable dishes, and practical advice on low-fat cooking in a wok.

Quick-fried Fish in Yellow Bean Sauce

Preparation time: 5 minutes, plus marinating
Cooking time: 5–6 minutes

Serves 3–4

4 tablespoons Fish Stock (see page 154)
3 tablespoons soy sauce
2 tablespoons yellow bean sauce
1 tablespoon rice wine or dry sherry
1 teaspoon caster sugar
500 g (1 lb) monkfish fillet, skinned and cut into
    chunks
1 tablespoon groundnut oil

1 Mix the stock, soy sauce, yellow bean sauce, rice wine or sherry and sugar in a shallow dish, add the monkfish and turn gently to coat. Cover and leave to marinate in the refrigerator for 1–2 hours, turning the fish occasionally.

2 Heat the oil in a wok. Add the fish and the marinade and stir-fry over a high heat for 4–5 minutes, or until the fish is tender. Serve immediately.

wok tip
Monkfish has a meaty flavour, firm flesh and no pin bones, so it is a good choice if you are uncertain how 'piscatorial' your guests are.

Rapid Fried Prawns

Preparation time: 10 minutes
Cooking time: 5 minutes

Serves 4

vegetable oil, for deep-frying
500 g (1 lb) raw tiger prawns, peeled and deveined,
    with tails left intact
2 teaspoons cornflour
1 tablespoon cold water

SWEET-AND-SOUR SAUCE:
2 tablespoons rice wine or dry sherry
2 tablespoons soy sauce
2 tablespoons wine or cider vinegar
1 tablespoon sugar
1 teaspoon finely chopped spring onion
1 teaspoon finely chopped fresh root ginger

1 Heat the oil in the wok to 180–190°C (350–375°F), or until a cube of bread browns in 30 seconds. Add the prawns and deep-fry until they turn bright pink. Lift them out with a slotted spoon and drain on kitchen paper.

2 Pour off all but 1 tablespoon of oil from the wok and increase the heat to high. Quickly mix together the sauce ingredients and add to the wok with the prawns. Cook for 1 minute, stirring constantly.

3 Mix the cornflour to a smooth paste with the water. Add to the wok and stir until all the prawns are coated with the sauce.

wok tip
This speedy but delicious dish is a great choice for an after-work supper with friends. Serve with fried rice or noodles.

Prawn Vermicelli

Preparation time: 10 minutes
Cooking time: 20 minutes

Serves 3–4

125 ml (4 fl oz, ½ cup) milk
1 teaspoon dark soy sauce
3 tablespoons oyster sauce
2 tablespoons vegetable oil
1 teaspoon chopped garlic
5 black peppercorns, crushed
1 tablespoon chopped fresh coriander leaf, stem and
    root
2 cm (¾ inch) piece of fresh root ginger, peeled and
    shredded
125 g (4 oz) cellophane noodles, soaked
12 large raw prawns, peeled and deveined, with tails
    left intact
fresh coriander leaves, to garnish

1 Combine the milk, soy sauce and oyster sauce in a bowl.

2 Heat the oil in a wok, add the garlic, peppercorns, coriander and ginger and stir-fry for 30 seconds. Add the noodles and the milk mixture, stir together thoroughly over a high heat, then reduce the heat to low, cover the wok, and cook for 12 minutes.

3 Finally, increase the heat, add the prawns and a little water, if the sauce looks too thick, and cook, stirring constantly, for about 2–3 minutes, until all the prawns have turned pink. Turn into a serving bowl and garnish with coriander leaves.

wok tip
To make Chicken Vermicelli, substitute 1 large boneless, skinless chicken breast for the prawns. Slice the chicken thinly and add to the wok with the noodles in step 2.

Scallops with Lemon and Ginger

Preparation time: 10 minutes
Cooking time: 10 minutes

Serves 2–4

8 large fresh scallops, shelled
3 tablespoons groundnut oil
½ bunch spring onions, thinly sliced
3 tablespoons lemon juice
2 tablespoons rice wine or dry sherry
2 pieces of stem ginger, chopped, with 1 tablespoon syrup from the jar
salt and pepper
lemon slices, to garnish

1 Slice the scallops thickly. Detach the corals and keep them whole. Heat 2 tablespoons of the oil in a wok. Add the white parts of the scallops and stir-fry over a moderate heat for 2 minutes, then transfer them to a plate with a slotted spoon.

2 Heat the remaining oil in the wok until hot. Add the spring onions and stir-fry for a few seconds, then add the lemon juice and rice wine or sherry and bring to the boil. Stir in the stem ginger and syrup.

3 Return the scallops and their juices to the wok and toss quickly over a high heat until heated through. Add the reserved corals and stir-fry for 30 seconds. Add salt and pepper to taste and serve immediately, garnished with lemon slices.

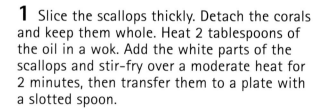

wok tip
The scallop is a very tender piece of seafood and needs only to be shown to the heat of the wok for an instant, in order to sear the outside. Never overcook.

Squid and Green Peppers

Preparation time: 15 minutes
Cooking time: 5 minutes

Serves 2–4

vegetable oil, for deep-frying
250 g (8 oz) prepared squid, thinly sliced
1 green pepper, cored, deseeded and sliced
2 slices fresh root ginger, peeled and shredded
1 teaspoon salt
1 tablespoon soy sauce
1 teaspoon rice vinegar
1 teaspoon sesame oil
pepper

wok tip
To save time, buy the squid ready prepared or ask your fishmonger to clean and prepare it for you.

1 Heat the oil in the wok to 180–190°C (350–375°F), or until a cube of bread browns in 30 seconds. Add the squid and deep-fry for 30 seconds, then remove with a slotted spoon and drain on kitchen paper. Carefully pour off the excess oil, leaving about 1 tablespoon in the wok.

2 Return the squid to the wok and add the green pepper and ginger. Stir-fry for a few seconds, then stir in the salt, soy sauce, vinegar and pepper. Cook for about 1 minute, then add the sesame oil and serve.

Cashew Chicken with Garlic, Wine and Ginger

Preparation time: 10 minutes
Cooking time: 3–4 minutes

Serves 4

375 g (12 oz) boneless, skinless chicken
1 egg white, lightly beaten
4 tablespoons rice wine or dry sherry
2 teaspoons cornflour
3 tablespoons sunflower oil
4 spring onions, chopped
2 garlic cloves, chopped
2.5 cm (1 inch) piece of fresh root ginger, peeled and finely chopped
1 tablespoon light soy sauce
125 g (4 oz, 1 cup) unsalted cashew nuts

1 Cut the chicken into 1 cm (½ inch) cubes. Mix together the egg white, half the rice wine or sherry and the cornflour in a shallow dish. Place the chicken cubes in this mixture and toss until evenly coated.

2 Heat the oil in a wok. Add the spring onions, garlic and ginger and stir-fry for 30 seconds. Add the chicken and stir-fry for 2 minutes or until cooked through.

3 Pour in the remaining wine and the soy sauce and stir well. Add the cashew nuts and cook for a further 30 seconds. Serve immediately.

wok tip
Cashew nuts are widely used in Chinese cooking, and are highly prized for their sweet, rich flavour. They are mostly used in chicken or in stir-fried vegetable dishes. Be sure to use unsalted nuts.

Ginger Chicken with Honey

Preparation time: 15 minutes, plus soaking
Cooking time: 10–15 minutes

Serves 4

50 g (2 oz, ⅓ cup) fresh root ginger, peeled and finely chopped
2 tablespoons vegetable oil
3 boneless, skinless chicken breasts, chopped
3 chicken livers, chopped
1 onion, thinly sliced
3 garlic cloves, crushed
2 tablespoons dried black fungus, soaked in hot water for 20 minutes
2 tablespoons soy sauce
1 tablespoon clear honey
5 spring onions, chopped
1 fresh red chilli, deseeded and thinly sliced into strips, to garnish
rice sticks, to serve (optional)

1 Mix the ginger with a little cold water, then drain and squeeze it dry.

2 Heat the oil in a wok and add the chicken breasts and livers. Stir-fry the chicken mixture over a moderate heat for 5 minutes, then remove it with a slotted spoon and set aside.

3 Add the onion to the wok and fry it gently until soft, then add the garlic and the drained black fungus and stir-fry for 1 minute. Return the chicken mixture to the wok and stir.

4 Mix together the soy sauce and honey in a bowl until blended, then pour this in to the wok and stir well. Add the drained ginger and stir-fry for 2–3 minutes. Finally, add the spring onions. Serve immediately, garnished with strips of red chilli and accompanied by rice sticks, if using.

wok tip
This dish tastes even better if it is cooked a day in advance and then thoroughly reheated before being served.

Stir-fried Sesame Chicken

Preparation time: 10 minutes
Cooking time: 10 minutes

Serves 3–4

500 g (1 lb) boneless, skinless chicken breast, cut into
    2.5 cm (1 inch) cubes
1½ teaspoons cornflour
4 tablespoons vegetable oil
1 green pepper, cored, deseeded and cut into 2.5 cm
    (1 inch) pieces
2½ tablespoons soy sauce
2½ tablespoons sesame seed paste
1 tablespoon sesame oil
1 tablespoon water
1 teaspoon chilli sauce
1 tablespoon rice wine or dry sherry
sesame seeds, to garnish

1 Put the chicken cubes into a bowl, sprinkle with the cornflour and toss until they are evenly coated. Heat the oil in a wok and add the chicken. Stir-fry over a high heat for 45 seconds, then remove from the wok with a slotted spoon and set aside.

2 Add the green pepper to the hot oil in the wok and stir-fry briskly over moderate heat for 1 minute. Stir in 1 tablespoon of the soy sauce, then remove the green pepper with a slotted spoon and set aside.

3 Add the remaining soy sauce, the sesame seed paste, sesame oil, water, chilli sauce and rice wine or sherry to the wok. Mix together well and cook for 1 minute.

4 Return the chicken cubes to the sauce mixture in the wok and stir over a high heat for about 45 seconds. Stir in the reserved green pepper. Cook for a further 30 seconds, until the pepper is just tender. Transfer to a serving dish and serve immediately, garnished with sesame seeds.

wok tip
Serve this strongly-flavoured dish with plain egg noodles, rice sticks or plain rice.

Fried Pork Balls

Preparation time: 15 minutes
Cooking time: 15 minutes

Serves 4

2 teaspoons chopped fresh coriander stems
2 teaspoons pepper
4 garlic cloves, peeled
pinch of sugar
500 g (1 lb) minced pork
2 tablespoons Thai fish sauce
plain flour, for coating
4–5 tablespoons vegetable oil
fresh coriander leaves, to garnish

1 Put the coriander stems, pepper, garlic and sugar into blender and process to a smooth paste. Alternatively, use a mortar and pestle.

2 Put the pork and the coriander paste into a food processor or blender and add the fish sauce. Process until the mixture is thick and smooth, then transfer to a bowl.

3 Form the mixture into about 20 small balls, about 2.5 cm (1 inch) in diameter. Roll the pork balls lightly in a little flour.

4 Heat the oil in a wok and add about 5 pork balls. Fry over moderate heat for 2–3 minutes, or until no liquid is released from the pork balls when they are pierced with a knife. Remove from the wok with a slotted spoon and drain on kitchen paper. Keep warm while you fry the remaining pork balls. Serve hot, garnished with coriander leaves.

wok tip
These pork balls can be served with a selection of stir-fried dishes and curries. Skewered on cocktail sticks, they also make a tempting appetizer with drinks.

Mangetout and Beef Stir-fry

Preparation time: 15 minutes, plus marinating
Cooking time: about 8 minutes

Serves 4

250 g (8 oz) rump steak, thinly sliced
2 tablespoons oyster sauce
1 tablespoon rice wine or dry sherry
1 teaspoon cornflour
4 tablespoons oil
2 spring onions, cut into 2.5 cm (1 inch) lengths
1 slice fresh root ginger, peeled and cut into strips
250 g (8 oz) mangetout, trimmed
1 teaspoon sugar
salt

1 Cut the beef slices into narrow strips and put in a
bowl with the oyster sauce, rice wine or sherry and
cornflour. Mix well, then leave to marinate for about 20
minutes.

2 Heat 2 tablespoons of the oil in a wok and stir-fry the
spring onions and ginger for a few seconds. Add the beef
and stir-fry until evenly browned. Transfer the mixture to
a warm serving dish and keep hot.

3 Heat the remaining oil in the wok and stir-fry the
mangetout, sugar and salt to taste for about 2 minutes.
Do not allow the mangetout to overcook, or they will
lose their texture and colour. Add the mangetout to the
beef and mix well. Serve immediately.

wok tip
As a variation, substitute 125 g
(4 oz) baby sweetcorn and 125 g
(4 oz) sugar snaps for the mangetout.
Cook for 2–3 minutes, mixing well.

Spring Lamb Stir-fried with Garlic

Preparation time: 5 minutes, plus marinating
Cooking time: 5–7 minutes

Serves 4

2 tablespoons rice wine or dry sherry
2 tablespoons light soy sauce
1 tablespoon dark soy sauce
1 teaspoon sesame oil
375 g (12 oz) lamb fillet, thinly sliced across the grain
2 tablespoons vegetable oil
6 garlic cloves, thinly sliced
2.5 cm (1 inch) piece of fresh root ginger, peeled and
  chopped
1 leek, thinly sliced diagonally
4 spring onions, chopped

1 Mix the rice wine or sherry with the soy sauces and sesame oil in a bowl. Add the lamb and toss to coat evenly on all sides. Cover and leave to marinate for 15 minutes.

2 Drain the lamb, reserving the marinade. Heat the vegetable oil in a wok. Add the meat with 2 teaspoons of the marinade and stir-fry briskly for about 2 minutes, or until the meat is well browned. Add a little extra marinade, if necessary, to prevent the meat from sticking.

3 Add the garlic, ginger, leek and spring onions and stir-fry for a further 3 minutes. Serve immediately.

wok tip
The lamb should be thinly sliced so that it cooks rapidly. It should be cut across the grain using a sharp knife. Placing the meat in a freezer for about 1 hour before slicing makes it firm and easier to cut.

Stir-fried Liver with Spinach and Ginger

Preparation time: 10 minutes
Cooking time: 4–5 minutes

Serves 4

375 g (12 oz) lambs' liver, thinly sliced
2 tablespoons cornflour
4 tablespoons sunflower oil
500 g (1 lb) spinach, washed and drained
1 teaspoon salt
2 thin slices fresh root ginger, peeled and chopped
1 tablespoon light soy sauce
1 tablespoon rice wine or dry sherry
finely chopped spring onion, to garnish

1 Blanch the slices of liver in boiling water for a few seconds. Drain and coat with cornflour.

2 Heat 2 tablespoons of the oil in a wok. Add the spinach and salt and stir-fry for 2 minutes. Remove from the wok and arrange around the edge of a warmed serving dish. Keep the spinach hot.

3 Wipe the wok clean with kitchen paper. Heat the remaining oil in the wok until very hot. Add the ginger, liver, soy sauce and rice wine or sherry. Stir briskly for 1–2 minutes – avoid overcooking or the liver will become tough. Pour the mixture over the spinach and garnish with spring onion.

wok tip
Blanching liver in boiling water is a good way of ensuring that it remains tender during the cooking process. This is a robust stir-fry, quickly prepared and cooked.

Stir-fried Mushrooms

Preparation time: 5 minutes, plus soaking
Cooking time: 10 minutes

Serves 4

1 tablespoon oil
1 teaspoon peeled and finely chopped fresh root
    ginger
2 spring onions, finely chopped
1 garlic clove, crushed
1 fresh red chilli, deseeded and finely chopped
125 g (4 oz) shiitake mushrooms
50 g (2 oz) oyster mushrooms
50 g (2 oz) Hon-shimeji mushrooms
250 g (8 oz) button mushrooms
1 teaspoon chilli bean paste or chilli powder
2 teaspoons rice wine or dry sherry
2 teaspoons dark soy sauce
1 tablespoon water
pinch of salt
pinch of sugar
1 teaspoon sesame oil

1 Heat the oil in a wok over a moderate heat. Add the ginger, spring onions, garlic and chilli and stir-fry briskly for 5–10 seconds.

2 Add all of the mushrooms to the wok and stir-fry for 5 minutes.

3 Add the chilli bean paste or chilli powder, rice wine or sherry, soy sauce, measured water, salt, sugar and sesame oil. Mix well, then cook, stirring constantly, for 5 minutes. Serve immediately.

wok tip

Dried shiitake mushrooms make a convenient alternative to fresh ones. Soak them in warm water for 20 minutes, drain, squeeze dry and discard the stalks. Add to the stir-fry with the other mushrooms.

Pak Choi with Garlic and Oyster Sauce

Preparation time: 10 minutes, plus soaking
Cooking time: 3 minutes

Serves 4

1 tablespoon fermented black beans
500 g (1 lb) pak choi, trimmed
3 tablespoons vegetable oil
2 garlic cloves, crushed
2 tablespoons soy sauce
3 tablespoons oyster sauce
4 tablespoons water
boiled rice, to serve

1 Rinse the black beans to get rid of any excess salt. Put them into a bowl of hot water and leave to soften for 10 minutes. Drain.

2 Roughly chop the larger pak choi leaves or quarter small leaves.

3 Heat the oil in a wok, add the garlic and stir-fry for 1 minute. Add the pak choi and stir to coat in the oil.

4 Mix the soy and oyster sauces with the measured water and add to the wok with the black beans. Stir-fry quickly over a high heat for 1 minute and serve with plain boiled rice.

wok tip
Stir-fried green vegetables with garlic and black beans are popular in China. Use pak choi, ung choi or choi sum but do not overcook them; the leaves should retain their crisp texture.

Stir-fried Mixed Vegetables

Preparation time: 10 minutes, plus soaking
Cooking time: 3–4 minutes

Serves 3–4

5–6 dried shiitake mushrooms or 50 g (2 oz) button
   mushrooms
250 g (8 oz) Chinese leaves, thinly sliced
175 g (6 oz, 1 cup) carrots, thinly sliced
125 g (4 oz) French beans, trimmed
4 tablespoons vegetable oil
1 teaspoon salt
1 teaspoon sugar
1 tablespoon light soy sauce

1 If you are using dried mushrooms, soak
them in warm water for 20 minutes, then
drain, squeeze dry and remove the tough
stalks. Thinly slice the mushrooms.

2 Heat the oil in a wok and add the Chinese
leaves and carrots. Stir-fry briskly for 30
seconds. Add the beans and mushrooms and
continue to stir-fry for 30 seconds.

3 Add the salt and sugar, then toss the
vegetables until well mixed. Stir in the soy
sauce and cook for 1 minute more. Transfer to
a warm serving dish and serve immediately.

wok tip
Many different vegetables
are suitable for this dish,
including broccoli, sugar snaps,
mangetout, bamboo shoots and
water chestnuts. This makes a good
accompaniment to a highly
flavoured meat or fish dish.

Low-fat wok-ing

On the whole Oriental cuisine is comparatively healthy if you use cooking methods like stir-frying and steaming and avoid heavy sauces. Typically it includes a lot of vegetables and fat-free condiments and does not rely heavily on dairy produce and red meat, which are high in saturated fats. However, it is worth knowing what steps you can take to make Oriental cooking even less fattening.

Reducing your fat intake

Most of us eat too much fat on a regular basis. This makes us more likely to be overweight and puts us at greater risk of heart disease, especially if we eat too much saturated fat (the type of fat found in milk and meat products, and in coconuts).

When it comes to Asian cooking, steamed and stir-fried dishes usually have the lowest fat content. As it uses only a little oil stir-frying is a relatively low-fat cooking method — reduce the amount of oil even further if you can, try using a low-calorie spray oil or even omit the oil completely if you have a nonstick wok.

Fat is often used to add flavour to dishes, so use more flavoursome ingredients such as garlic, chilli, coriander, pepper and ginger in your cooking instead. Avoid obviously fatty dishes, for example deep-fried dishes like fried wontons, crispy seaweed, sweet and sour pork and spring rolls. If you must eat spring rolls and wontons, you can get rid of some of the excess fat by rolling them on kitchen paper or a paper napkin before eating to soak up some of the grease.

You should also avoid dishes containing lots of nuts, coconut cream or coconut milk if you want to reduce your fat intake. If you don't want to miss them out altogether, reduce the quantity of nuts in the recipe and use reduced-fat coconut milk in your cooking. In recipes like stir-fried rice that use several eggs, replace one or two whole eggs with just egg whites for a lower-fat version of the recipe.

Rice and noodles

Always opt for plain steamed or boiled rice rather than egg-fried rice. Plain rice is low in calories and a good starchy carbohydrate food. If you fill up on rice, you are less likely to eat too much of the more fattening dishes.

Plain noodles are also a good low-calorie choice and there are many varieties to choose from. Noodle-based dishes like chow mein are low in saturated fat — opt for vegetables, chicken or prawns to accompany the noodles for the healthiest option. Steer clear of dishes with fried noodles, however.

10 Low-fat tips

1 Cook with ingredients with a low-fat content where possible, for example low-fat natural yogurt and reduced-fat coconut milk.

2 Choose dishes with a high proportion of vegetables to meat.

3 Opt for boiled or steamed rice rather than egg-fried rice.

4 Never overcook stir-fried food. Use only a little oil for stir-frying or use a nonstick wok.

5 Avoid deep-fried dishes.

6 Avoid dishes with nuts, coconut milk or cream.

7 Steer clear of dishes with heavy sauces, for example red-braised Chinese dishes (see page 9), which are simmered in dark soy sauce and sugar.

8 Remove the batter from batter-fried ingredients like sweet and sour pork.

9 Eat using chopsticks — you are more likely to leave excess sauce and nuts in your bowl. It also makes you eat more slowly so that you feel fuller earlier (it takes 20 minutes for the brain to register that your stomach is full).

10 It's tempting to overeat with an Asian buffet-style meal — know when to stop and always refuse second helpings!

Meat, fish and vegetables

Reduce the amount of meat you eat by opting for more vegetable dishes than meat-based ones, or for dishes with a high proportion of vegetables to meat. Choose low-fat protein like chicken, turkey, prawns or scallops in preference to red meat, or try vegetarian alternatives like tofu. Always remove the skin from poultry and trim the fat off meat — partially freezing the meat before cutting makes it easier both to slice and to remove the fat, but let it thaw fully before cooking.

Not only are vegetables low-fat and low-calorie foods, they also help fill you up and so indirectly stop you eating more fattening foods. Stir-fried or steamed vegetable dishes are probably the healthiest options of all Asian-style foods in terms of saturated fat content.

chapter 3
Stars of the East

A selection of all-time favourites, including
Cantonese Pork in Sweet-and-sour Sauce,
Kashmiri Chicken, Laksa and Chow Mein,
plus all you need to know about
authentic Oriental ingredients.

Potstickers

Preparation time: 30 minutes, plus chilling
Cooking time: about 25 minutes

Serves 3–4

12–16 round Wonton Wrappers (see page 157)
2 tablespoons groundnut oil
400 ml (14 fl oz, 1¾ cups) hot Chicken Stock (see page 154)
soy sauce and Chilli Sauce (see page 156), to serve

FILLING:
8 raw tiger prawns, peeled and deveined
2 spring onions, quartered crossways
1 garlic clove, halved
2.5 cm (1 inch) piece of fresh root ginger, peeled and sliced
1 teaspoon light soy sauce
½ teaspoon rice wine vinegar
salt and pepper

1 Put all the filling ingredients in a food processor fitted with a metal blade. Add a pinch each of salt and pepper and process until finely minced. Turn the mixture into a bowl, cover and chill in the refrigerator for about 30 minutes, until firm.

2 Place the wonton wrappers on a work surface. Heap about ½ teaspoon of the filling on each wrapper, placing it slightly off centre. Brush all around the edges of the wrappers with water. Fold the empty side of each wrapper over the mound of filling, making three pleats in it as you go. Press the rounded edges to seal in the filling, then pleat all around the rounded edges to make an attractive crimped finish. There is enough filling to make 12 quite plump dumplings, but if you find them difficult to make with so much filling, use less filling and make 16 dumplings.

3 Heat 1 tablespoon of the oil in a wok until hot. Place half of the potstickers flat-side down in the hot oil and fry, without stirring or turning, for about 2 minutes, until

browned on the underside. Pour in half of the stock; this should be enough just to cover the potstickers. Bring to the boil, then lower the heat and simmer for about 10 minutes, until the stock has been absorbed into the potstickers. Repeat with the remaining oil, potstickers and stock. Serve hot, with soy sauce and chilli sauce for dipping.

wok tip
These little dumplings take their name from the fact that they stick to the pan during cooking. The wonton pastry is first fried, then cooked in stock. The end result is pleasantly chewy and full of flavour.

Szechuan Scallops

Preparation time: 15 minutes
Cooking time: 10 minutes

Serves 4

2 tablespoons vegetable oil
750 g (1½ lb) shelled large fresh scallops
2 garlic cloves, crushed
1 dried red chilli, finely chopped
½ teaspoon Chinese five-spice powder
2.5 cm (1 inch) piece of fresh root ginger, peeled and finely
    shredded
2 tablespoons rice wine or dry sherry
2 tablespoons dark soy sauce
3 tablespoons water
6 spring onions, diagonally sliced, plus extra to garnish
1 small onion, sliced
1 teaspoon caster sugar

1 Heat the oil in a wok until smoking hot. Add the
scallops and sear on both sides, remove and reserve.

2 Add the garlic, chilli, five-spice powder and ginger to
the wok and stir-fry for 1 minute. Add the rice wine or
sherry, soy sauce, measured water, spring onions, onion
and caster sugar and stir-fry for 1 minute, then return
the scallops to the wok and stir-fry them in the sauce for
2 minutes only.

3 Arrange the scallops with their sauce on a warmed
serving dish and garnish with spring onions.

wok tip
Food from the region of
Szechuan, in western China, is
hot and spicy. Chilli, ginger, onion
and garlic are used liberally and are
in great evidence in this fiery
scallop dish.

Malaysian Orange Chicken

Preparation time: 15 minutes
Cooking time: 10–15 minutes

Serves 4

2 egg whites
2 tablespoons cornflour
4 boneless, skinless chicken breasts, cut across the
   grain into thin strips
about 300 ml (½ pint, 1¼ cups) vegetable oil
1 bunch of spring onions, thinly sliced diagonally
125 g (4 oz, 1 cup) fresh or frozen peas
salt and pepper

SAUCE:
175 ml (6 fl oz, ¾ cup) orange juice
3–4 tablespoons concentrated orange squash
2 tablespoons soy sauce
1 tablespoon cider vinegar
1 teaspoon soft brown sugar

TO GARNISH:
orange slices
fresh flat leaf parsley

1 Using a fork, lightly whisk the egg whites with the cornflour and a pinch of salt in a shallow dish. Add the chicken and turn the strips to coat them evenly. Mix all the ingredients for the sauce and set aside.

2 Heat the oil in a wok until hot, but not smoking. Use a fork to add the strips of chicken individually to the hot oil. Fry for 3–4 minutes, or until golden – you will have to do this in batches. Use a slotted spoon to remove the chicken and drain on kitchen paper. Keep hot.

3 Pour off almost all the oil from the wok. Add the spring onions and stir-fry briskly over a moderate heat for 30 seconds. Pour in the sauce and bring to the boil, stirring, then add the peas and salt and pepper to taste. Simmer, stirring frequently, for about 5 minutes, or until the peas are cooked.

4 Return the chicken to the wok and toss for 1–2 minutes, or until all the ingredients are well combined and piping hot. Serve garnished with orange slices and flat leaf parsley.

wok tip
You can reuse the oil once or twice, so don't throw it away after pouring it out of the wok in step 3. Let it go cold, then strain and pour into a bottle.

Thai Green Chicken Curry

Preparation time: 10 minutes
Cooking time: 25 minutes

Serves 4

2 tablespoons groundnut oil
2.5 cm (1 inch) piece of fresh root ginger, peeled and
   finely chopped
2 shallots, chopped
4 tablespoons Green Curry Paste (see page 155)
625 g (1¼ lb) boneless, skinless chicken thighs, cut
   into 5 cm (2 inch) pieces
300 ml (½ pint, 1¼ cups) Coconut Milk (see page 156)
4 tablespoons Thai fish sauce
1 teaspoon palm sugar or light brown sugar
3 kaffir lime leaves, finely chopped
1 fresh green chilli, deseeded and thinly sliced
salt and pepper
Crispy Fried Garlic (see page 157), to garnish
rice sticks, to serve (optional)

1 Heat the oil in a wok. Add the ginger and
shallots and stir-fry over a low heat for about
3 minutes, or until softened. Add the curry
paste and fry for 2 minutes.

2 Add the chicken to the wok, stir until

wok tip
This traditional Thai dish
can be made with a variety of
other ingredients, such as duck, fish
and prawns. Duck should be cooked
in exactly the same way as chicken,
but add fish or prawns to the
curry in step 3.

evenly coated in the spice mixture and fry for
3 minutes to seal the chicken pieces. Stir in
the coconut milk and bring the curry to the
boil. Reduce the heat and cook the curry over
a low heat, stirring occasionally, for about 10
minutes, or until the chicken is cooked
through and the sauce has thickened.

3 Stir in the fish sauce, sugar, kaffir lime
leaves and chilli. Cook the curry for a further 5
minutes, then add salt and pepper to taste.
Garnish the curry with crispy fried garlic and
serve rice sticks as an accompaniment, if liked.

Kashmiri Chicken

Preparation time: 10 minutes
Cooking time: about 40 minutes

Serves 4–6

50 g (2 oz, ¼ cup) ghee or butter
3 large onions, thinly sliced
10 peppercorns
10 cardamom pods
5 cm (2 inch) piece of cinnamon stick
5 cm (2 inch) piece of fresh root ginger, peeled and
    chopped
2 garlic cloves, finely chopped
1 teaspoon chilli powder
2 teaspoons paprika
1.5 kg (3 lb) skinless chicken pieces
250 ml (8 fl oz, 1 cup) natural yogurt
salt

TO GARNISH:
lime wedges
chopped fresh parsley

1 Melt the ghee or butter in a wok. Add the onions, peppercorns, cardamoms and cinnamon and fry for about 8–10 minutes, stirring occasionally, until the onions are golden.

2 Add the ginger, garlic, chilli powder, paprika and salt to taste and fry for 2 minutes, stirring occasionally.

3 Add the chicken pieces and fry until they are evenly browned. Gradually add the yogurt, stirring constantly. Cover and cook for about 30 minutes, or until the chicken is cooked through. Serve hot, garnished with lime wedges and parsley.

wok tip
Serve this rich and delicious curry with plain boiled rice or plain breads, such as chappatis.

Bang Bang Chicken

Preparation time: 30 minutes, plus marinating and cooling
Cooking time: about 15 minutes

Serves 4

4 boneless, skinless chicken breasts
6 tablespoons soy sauce
2 tablespoons sesame oil
2.5 cm (1 inch) piece of fresh root ginger, peeled and finely chopped
4 tablespoons vegetable oil
4 carrots, cut into matchsticks
1 fresh green or red chilli, deseeded and chopped
125 g (4 oz) bean sprouts
½ cucumber, cut into matchsticks
3 tablespoons rice wine or dry sherry
2 tablespoons clear honey
150 ml (¼ pint, ⅔ cup) Chicken Stock (see page 154)
2 tablespoons sesame seeds, toasted
fresh flat leaf parsley, to garnish

wok tip
To toast the sesame seeds, heat a wok or frying pan until hot. Dry-fry the sesame seeds over a gentle heat for 1–2 minutes, tossing so that they do not burn. Tip the seeds on to a plate to cool.

1 Place the chicken breasts between 2 sheets of greaseproof paper and bang hard with a rolling pin to flatten and tenderize them. Cut the chicken into thin strips across the grain, then place in a shallow dish. Mix 2 tablespoons of the soy sauce with the sesame oil and ginger. Pour the mixture over the chicken and turn to coat. Cover and leave to marinate for 20 minutes, turning occasionally.

2 Meanwhile, heat 2 tablespoons of the vegetable oil in a wok over a moderate heat. Add the carrots and chilli and stir-fry for 2–3 minutes. Remove with a slotted spoon and place in a bowl. Add the bean sprouts to the wok and stir-fry for 1 minute, then tip the bean sprouts into the bowl. Add the cucumber sticks to the bowl and toss well.

3 Heat the remaining oil in the wok. Add the chicken, increase the heat and stir-fry for 4–5 minutes. Transfer the chicken to a separate bowl.

4 Add the remaining soy sauce, the rice wine or sherry, honey and stock to the wok. Bring to the boil, stirring, then simmer for a few minutes, stirring constantly, until reduced slightly. Pour half of the sauce mixture over the vegetables and half over the chicken. Stir to mix, then cover and leave to cool, stirring occasionally.

5 Arrange the chicken and vegetables on individual plates, drizzle over any sauce remaining in the bowls and sprinkle with the sesame seeds. Garnish with parsley and serve.

Cantonese Pork in Sweet-and-sour Sauce

wok tip
Chinese five-spice powder has a sweet aromatic quality which goes particularly well with pork and chicken. You don't need much or you will overpower the dish.

Preparation time: 10 minutes
Cooking time: 20–30 minutes

Serves 4–6

500 g (1 lb) pork fillet, cut into 2.5 cm (1 inch) cubes
1 teaspoon salt
pinch of pepper
½ teaspoon Chinese five-spice powder
2 tablespoons rice wine or dry sherry
1 egg
3 tablespoons cornflour
vegetable oil, for deep-frying
1 garlic clove, crushed
1 onion, roughly chopped
1–2 green peppers, cored, deseeded and diced
250 g (8 oz) can pineapple chunks in juice, drained and juice reserved
3 tablespoons wine vinegar
50 g (2 oz, ¼ cup) sugar
4 tablespoons tomato ketchup

1 Fill a saucepan with water and bring to the boil. Add the pork and boil until it changes colour. Drain the pork, cool and pat dry with kitchen paper.

2 Mix together the salt, pepper, five-spice powder, rice wine or sherry, egg and cornflour. Add the pork and turn to coat well.

3 Heat the oil in a wok to 180–190°C (350–375°F), or until a cube of bread browns in 30 seconds. Deep-fry the pork, in batches, until brown. Drain thoroughly on kitchen paper.

4 Carefully pour off the oil, leaving just 2 tablespoons in the wok. Add the garlic and fry until golden. Add the onion and green peppers, and stir-fry for 1 minute. Stir in the pineapple juice with the vinegar, sugar and tomato ketchup.

5 Cook, stirring, until thickened. Add the pork and stir until heated through. Serve hot, garnished with the pineapple chunks.

Special Egg-fried Rice

Preparation time: 10 minutes
Cooking time: 8–10 minutes

Serves 4

2–3 eggs
2 spring onions, finely chopped, plus extra to garnish
2 teaspoons salt
3 tablespoons vegetable oil
125 g (4 oz) cooked peeled prawns
125 g (4 oz) cooked chicken or pork, diced
50 g (2 oz, $\frac{1}{3}$ cup) bamboo shoots, roughly chopped
4 tablespoons fresh or frozen peas, cooked
1 tablespoon light soy sauce
375–500 g (12 oz–1 lb, 5–7 cups) cold cooked rice

1 Break the eggs into a small bowl and add 1 teaspoon of the spring onions and a pinch of the salt. Beat lightly together with a fork to combine.

2 Heat about 1 tablespoon of the oil in the wok and add the beaten egg mixture. Stir constantly until the eggs are scrambled and set. Remove the scrambled eggs from the wok and set aside in a bowl.

3 Heat the remaining oil in the wok and add the prawns, meat, bamboo shoots, peas and the remaining spring onions. Stir-fry briskly for 1 minute, then stir in the soy sauce.

4 Stir-fry for 2–3 minutes. Add the cooked rice with the scrambled eggs and the remaining salt. Stir well to break up the scrambled eggs into small pieces and to separate the grains of rice.

wok tip
All sorts of ingredients can be added to this dish and it is a great recipe for using up leftover cooked meat and vegetables. Try adding diced ham, chicken, beef, pork or turkey, shredded cabbage or canned water chestnuts.

Burmese Coconut Rice

Preparation time: 10 minutes
Cooking time: 25 minutes

Serves 4–6

500 g (1 lb) basmati rice
475 ml (16 fl oz, 2 cups) Coconut Milk (see page
   156)
1 onion, halved and sliced
2 teaspoons caster sugar
½ teaspoon salt
sesame seasoning (see wok tip), to serve

1 Place the rice, coconut milk, onion, sugar
and salt in a wok and tap the wok to level the
surface of the rice. Cover with enough water
to reach 2.5 cm (1 inch) above the rice. Bring
to the boil, then reduce the heat, cover with a
lid and simmer very gently for 20 minutes,
adding a little extra water if necessary, and
carefully stirring the rice once or twice to
prevent it from sticking to the base of the pan.

2 To serve, fluff up the rice with a fork and
sprinkle with a little sesame seasoning.

wok tip
For the sesame seasoning,
heat a dry wok, add 4 tablespoons
of sesame seeds and 1 teaspoon of
salt and dry-fry for 4 minutes,
stirring constantly. Remove from
the heat once the sesame seeds
are golden brown.

Laksa

Preparation time: 25 minutes
Cooking time: 20–25 minutes

Serves 4

3 tablespoons groundnut oil
2 large onions, finely chopped
4 garlic cloves, crushed
3 small fresh red chillies, deseeded and finely chopped
75 g (3 oz, ½ cup) Crushed Roasted Peanuts (see page 157), plus
   extra to serve
1 tablespoon ground coriander
1 tablespoon ground cumin
2 teaspoons ground turmeric
1.2 litres (2 pints, 5 cups) Coconut Milk (see page 156)
1 teaspoon shrimp paste
1–2 tablespoons sugar
375 g (12 oz) cooked chicken, shredded
175 g (6 oz) bean sprouts
500 g (1 lb) fresh noodles
4 spring onions, chopped, plus extra to serve
3 tablespoons chopped fresh coriander leaves
salt and pepper
1 large fresh red chilli, deseeded and thinly sliced, to serve

1 Heat the oil in a wok and fry the onions until golden brown. Add the garlic, chopped chillies, peanuts, ground coriander, cumin and turmeric and fry for 2–3 minutes, or until the spices have cooked through and released their aroma.

2 Stir in the coconut milk and shrimp paste, cover and simmer for 15 minutes. Season the spiced coconut with salt, pepper and sugar to taste. Add the shredded chicken and half of the bean sprouts and simmer for a further 5 minutes.

3 Blanch the noodles in boiling water and divide between 4 large bowls. Sprinkle with the spring onions and chopped coriander and divide the remaining raw bean sprouts between the bowls.

4 Ladle the chicken and coconut mixture over the noodles and serve with chopped spring onions, sliced red chilli and roasted peanuts.

wok tip
This rich and creamy coconut dish is made with fine cellophane noodles in the Philippines and flat rice noodles in Malaysia. If you can't get fresh noodles, use dry noodles instead.

Chow Mein

Preparation time: 10 minutes
Cooking time: 5–8 minutes

Serves 4

500 g (1 lb) dried egg noodles
4 tablespoons vegetable oil
1 onion, thinly sliced
125 g (4 oz) cooked pork, chicken or ham, cut into thin shreds
125 g (4 oz) mangetout or French beans, trimmed
125 g (4 oz) bean sprouts
2–3 spring onions, finely shredded
2 tablespoons light soy sauce
1 tablespoon sesame oil or chilli sauce
salt

1 Cook the noodles in a large pan of salted, boiling water according to packet instructions. Drain and rinse under cold running water until cool. Set aside.

2 Heat about 3 tablespoons of the oil in a wok. Add the onion, meat, mangetout or beans and the bean sprouts and stir-fry for about 1 minute. Add salt to taste and stir a few more times, then remove the mixture from the wok with a slotted spoon and keep hot.

3 Heat the remaining oil in the wok and add the spring onions and the noodles, together with about half the meat and vegetable mixture. Stir in the soy sauce, then stir-fry for 1–2 minutes, or until heated through.

4 Transfer the mixture from the wok to 4 warm serving bowls, then arrange the remaining meat and vegetable mixture on top. Sprinkle with sesame oil or chilli sauce (or both, if preferred) and serve immediately.

wok tip
To make vegetarian Chow Mein, substitute 1 finely sliced green pepper for the meat. Add 175 g (6 oz, 1½ cups) each of shredded Chinese leaves and whole baby spinach 1–2 minutes before serving.

Singapore Noodles

Preparation time: 25 minutes
Cooking time: 15 minutes

Serves 4

wok tip
Char siu roasted pork is authentic in this dish, and can be made at home or bought in a Chinese supermarket. Chinese bacon, plain roasted pork or cooked ham could be used instead.

2 tablespoons vegetable oil
1 onion, chopped
3 garlic cloves, crushed
2 tablespoons black bean sauce, plus extra to serve
2 tablespoons rice wine or dry sherry
1 fresh red chilli, deseeded and finely chopped
½ teaspoon Chinese five-spice powder
600 ml (1 pint, 2½ cups) Chicken Stock (see page 154) or water
250 g (8 oz) fresh egg noodles
150 g (5 oz) bean sprouts
250 g (8 oz) roasted pork, sliced
125 g (4 oz, 1 cup) pak choi, roughly chopped
125 g (4 oz) raw tiger prawns, peeled and deveined
salt

TO SERVE:
6 Crispy Fried Shallots (see page 157)
2 egg omelette, thinly shredded
2 fresh red chillies, deseeded and diagonally sliced
fresh coriander leaves
Chilli Sauce (see page 156)

1 Heat the oil in a wok, add the onion and stir-fry until beginning to brown. Add the garlic, black bean sauce, rice wine or sherry, chilli and five-spice powder and stir-fry for 2 minutes.

2 Add the stock or water, noodles and bean sprouts and bring to the boil, tossing the noodles and bean sprouts in the stock.

3 Add the pork to the wok with the pak choi, prawns and salt to taste and stir-fry for a further 4 minutes. Serve topped with the crispy fried shallots, shredded omelette, sliced chillies and coriander leaves and accompanied by the chilli sauce.

Thai Fried Noodles

Preparation time: 15 minutes, plus soaking
Cooking time: 20–25 minutes

Serves 2

3 tablespoons groundnut oil
175 g (6 oz, 1 cup) fried tofu, diced
1 tablespoon chopped garlic
125 g (4 oz) cellophane noodles, soaked and drained
25 g (1 oz, ¼ cup) carrot, grated
2 tablespoons distilled white vinegar or rice wine
   vinegar
2 tablespoons soy sauce
100 ml (3½ fl oz, ½ cup) water
2 eggs
3 teaspoons sugar
2 spring onions, sliced
½ teaspoon pepper

TO SERVE:
1 tablespoon Crushed Roasted Peanuts (see page 157)
125 g (4 oz) bean sprouts
1 spring onion, halved lengthways

1 Heat 2 tablespoons of the oil in a wok. Stir-fry the tofu until brown on all sides. Then stir in the garlic, noodles, carrot, vinegar, soy sauce and measured water.

2 Push the mixture to one side of the wok and add the eggs. Break the yolks and stir the eggs, gradually incorporating the noodle mixture.

3 Pour the remaining oil down the side of the wok and add the sugar, spring onions and pepper. Cook for 2–3 minutes, stirring and shaking the wok constantly.

4 Heap the noodle mixture on to a plate. Sprinkle the peanuts on top and serve with the bean sprouts and spring onion halves.

wok tip
To make this dish a little more substantial, add a few chopped vegetables, such as small broccoli florets, mangetout or fine French beans with the tofu and stir-fry briefly to soften.

Shanghai Stir-fry

Preparation time: about 20 minutes
Cooking time: about 8 minutes

Serves 4–6

4 tablespoons ready-made sweet-and-sour sauce
225 g (7½ oz) can pineapple chunks in juice
2 tablespoons vegetable oil
2 carrots, cut into matchsticks
1 fennel bulb, thinly sliced, with any leaves reserved
1 red pepper, cored, deseeded and cut lengthways into
    thin strips
1 green pepper, cored, deseeded and cut lengthways
    into thin strips
125 g (4 oz) bean sprouts
175 g (6 oz, 1½ cups) Chinese leaves, shredded
salt and pepper
chopped nuts (cashews, macadamias or peanuts), to
    garnish

1 Dilute the sweet-and-sour sauce with 3 tablespoons of pineapple juice from the can and set aside. Drain the pineapple and discard the remaining juice.

2 Heat the oil in a wok over a moderate heat. Add the carrots, fennel and red and green peppers and stir-fry for 3–4 minutes, until the vegetables are just beginning to soften.

3 Pour the diluted sweet-and-sour sauce into the wok, increase the heat to high and stir-fry until the mixture is bubbling. Add the pineapple chunks and bean sprouts and stir-fry for 1 minute, or until hot, then add the Chinese leaves and toss for 1 further minute, or until all the ingredients are well combined and piping hot. Add salt and pepper to taste and serve immediately, sprinkled with the chopped nuts and any reserved fennel leaves.

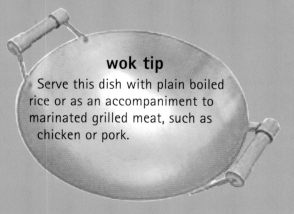

wok tip
Serve this dish with plain boiled rice or as an accompaniment to marinated grilled meat, such as chicken or pork.

Essential ingredients

Baby sweetcorn cobs
These delicious, finger-sized corn cobs are pale yellow in colour with a delicate, sweet flavour. Perfect for stir-fries, they can also be lightly boiled and served as a vegetable.

Bamboo shoots
These are the young, ivory-coloured, conical-shaped shoots of edible bamboo plants. They are tender and slightly crunchy and add sweetness to dishes. They are available canned and occasionally vacuum-packed.

Bean sprouts
These are sprouted mung beans. Fresh bean sprouts are by far the best, as canned ones are not as crunchy. Cook them quickly to preserve their texture. Fresh bean sprouts do not store well, so use them soon after buying them.

Chillies
There are so many different types of chilli that it would be impossible to list them all. As a general rule, the smaller the chilli the fiercer the heat, and red chillies are slightly less hot than green. Most of the heat in chillies is contained in the membranes around the seeds, so if you deseed them, you reduce the heat considerably.

Chinese leaves
These crisp, pale green leaves resemble a long, slim, tapering cabbage. They have a clean, delicate flavour and can be used in salads, stir-fries or braised dishes.

Coconut milk and cream
These are widely available in cans, packets and blocks (which require added water). You can also make your own (see page 156). Fresh coconut milk lasts only 1–2 days, even in the refrigerator. If you are using coconut cream, stir it constantly while cooking as it curdles easily.

Coriander
An essential ingredient in Thai cooking, all of this pungent herb is used, including the leaves, stems and roots. It can be bought fresh in most supermarkets.

Galangal
This is a root similar to ginger, but the skin is thinner and slightly pink, and the taste is more mellow. It is available in large supermarkets and Asian food shops. It is used and stored in the same way as ginger. Ground dried galangal is called laos powder, but the flavour is not so good as fresh galangal. Use fresh root ginger if you can't get galangal.

Garlic
Wok cookery relies on the use of garlic as an essential flavouring. Fresh garlic is by far the best and the cloves may be used whole, chopped or crushed. Garlic should be kept in a cool, dry place – if it is kept too long in the refrigerator, it may go mouldy or start to sprout.

Ginger
Fresh root ginger is readily available and is widely used in South-east Asian cooking for its piquant flavour. Choose plump roots with unwrinkled skin. It is peeled before use, then sliced, chopped or grated depending on the recipe. Sliced or chopped ginger can be kept in an airtight container in the refrigerator for up to 2 weeks. It also freezes well.

Kaffir lime leaves
These can be bought fresh or dried in Asian food shops or large supermarkets. They are the leaves from the kaffir

lime plant, also known as makrut, which grows in South-east Asia. If they are unavailable, use a strip of pared lime rind or a squeeze of lime juice instead.

Lemon grass
Now quite widely available in supermarkets, lemon grass is the stalk of a grass-like plant with an intense lemon flavour. The tough, outer leaves should be removed as well as the ends, and it can either be finely sliced or used whole, depending on the recipe. If used whole, the lemon grass is removed from the dish before serving. As a substitute, use a piece of pared lemon rind or a squeeze of lemon juice.

Noodles
There are many different kinds of noodles, but the most commonly available are egg noodles, rice vermicelli, rice sticks and cellophane noodles. Egg noodles can be bought fresh from Chinese food shops, but the dried ones found in supermarkets are just as good. Rice vermicelli are very thin, white and slightly transparent. They are made from rice and dried in long bundles, but can be cut into shorter lengths. Rice sticks are similar to rice vermicelli, only flatter and wider. Occasionally they can be found fresh (sold as *ho fun*) in Chinese supermarkets. Cellophane noodles, also known as glass noodles and bean thread noodles, are like rice vermicelli, but are made from mung beans instead of rice.

Pak choi
There are many different Chinese greens, including pak choi, ung choi and choi sum – and they are virtually interchangeable. Many are now available from supermarkets or specialist shops; use whatever is available. As an alternative, use Chinese leaves.

Papaya
Also called pawpaw, this tropical fruit can be bought in supermarkets and good greengrocers. When unripe, the pale green flesh is used in salads, but the ripe orange flesh is much sweeter and more aromatic.

Spring roll wrappers
White and flimsy, these are made from flour and water and can be either round or square in shape. Buy them ready-made in Chinese supermarkets, fresh or frozen in bags. They are very delicate, so handle them gently. If you can't find the size or shape you need, buy whatever is available and cut them to size. Rice paper spring roll wrappers are dried and become moist and flexible when they are brushed with egg or egg white. If spring roll wrappers are unavailable, use sheets of filo pastry instead and cut them to the size required.

Tofu
Made from soya beans, tofu is highly nutritious and readily absorbs other flavours, making a versatile addition to the diet. There are several kinds available and it is also known as bean curd. Fresh white tofu is sold in blocks in its own liquid. It is very delicate and will break up if stirred too much. Ready-fried or yellow tofu is sold in golden-brown cubes which are much more solid. They are ideal for stir-frying. You can also buy fairly solid white tofu cakes packed in water in plastic containers – these can be used for stir-frying if you can't get yellow tofu.

Water chestnuts
Available in cans and occasionally fresh, water chestnuts are white nuts with a brown skin. They are technically the corms from a species of water grass. Water chestnuts have a crunchy texture and sweet flavour, even when cooked. The Chinese use them extensively, both in cooked dishes and salads. Canned water chestnuts don't have much flavour, but their texture is still wonderfully crisp.

Wonton wrappers
Sometimes labelled 'dumpling pastries', these are sold in small plastic packets in the refrigerator or freezer sections of Chinese supermarkets. You can buy both round and square wrappers in different sizes. If you can't obtain exactly what you want, buy whatever you can and cut to shape or size. Made from wheat flour, egg and water, wonton wrappers are yellowish in colour, unlike spring roll wrappers which are pure white. You can substitute filo pastry or can make your own wonton wrappers at home (see page 157).

chapter 4
Hale and Hearty

Deep-frying, boiling, steaming and simmering – this chapter shows you how to make substantial and flavoursome dishes using a variety of wok techniques. There is also a guide to wok cooking for vegetarians.

Wheat Noodle Soup with Marinated Chicken

wok tip
Roast the peanuts and rice separately. Heat a dry frying pan, then add the peanuts or rice and cook until golden, stirring frequently.

Preparation time: 25 minutes
Cooking time: 30 minutes

Serves 4–6

300 g (10 oz) boneless, skinless chicken breast
1 teaspoon ground turmeric
2 teaspoons salt
2 lemon grass stalks
3 tablespoons peanuts, skinned and roasted
3 tablespoons white long-grain rice, roasted
2 tablespoons vegetable oil
1 onion, chopped
3 garlic cloves, crushed
5 cm (2 inch) piece of fresh root ginger, peeled and finely
   chopped
½ teaspoon paprika
2 small fresh red chillies, deseeded and chopped
2–3 tablespoons Thai fish sauce, plus extra to serve
900 ml (1½ pints, 3¾ cups) water
250 g (8 oz) wheat noodles (somen)

TO SERVE:
3 hard-boiled eggs, halved
3 tablespoons chopped fresh coriander leaves
3 spring onions, finely chopped
crushed dried chilli

1 Cut the chicken breasts into 2.5 cm (1 inch) cubes. Mix the turmeric with the salt, rub into the cubes of chicken and leave to stand for 30 minutes.

2 Bruise the lemon grass with the side of a rolling pin to release the flavour. Finely crush the roasted peanuts in a food processor or using a pestle and mortar. Finely crush the rice to a powder in a food processor or spice grinder.

3 Heat the oil in a wok and fry the onion until just softened. Add the dry marinated chicken together with the garlic, ginger, lemon grass, paprika and fresh chillies. Stir in the fish sauce and water and bring to the boil.

4 Reduce the heat and simmer gently. Mix the crushed peanuts and ground rice and add to the pan. Simmer for about 10–15 minutes, or until the chicken has cooked through and the broth has thickened slightly.

5 Bring a pan of water to the boil and cook the wheat noodles for 3–4 minutes or according to the packet instructions, until just tender. Drain and refresh with cold water and then divide between large soup bowls.

6 Ladle the chicken soup over the noodles and serve topped with the hard-boiled eggs, chopped coriander and spring onions. Add an extra splash of fish sauce and a sprinkling of crushed dried chilli, to taste. Eat the soup with a spoon and fork.

Vietnamese Dumplings

Preparation time: 25 minutes plus cooling
Cooking time: 10–15 minutes

Serves 4–6

500 g (1 lb) lean minced pork
2 tablespoons dried black fungus, soaked and finely chopped
2 small shallots, finely chopped
2 garlic cloves, crushed
1 fresh green chilli, deseeded and finely chopped
25 g (1 oz) coriander leaves and stalks
1 teaspoon salt
1 teaspoon pepper
2 tablespoons vegetable oil
1 tablespoon cornflour
2 tablespoons water
20–24 Wonton Wrappers (see page 157)
Soy and Vinegar Dipping Sauce (see page 156), to serve

TO GARNISH:
Crispy Fried Shallots (see page 157)
cucumber sticks

1 Mix the pork, black fungus, shallots, garlic, chilli, coriander, salt and pepper in a bowl.

2 Heat the oil in a wok and stir-fry the pork mixture for about 5 minutes, or until cooked through. Set aside until it is cool enough to handle.

3 Mix together the cornflour and water to a smooth paste in a small bowl, adding a little more water if necessary.

4 With your finger, paint some of the cornflour mixture around the edge of a wonton wrapper. Put a teaspoon of the pork mixture on the wrapper in a sausage shape. Roll up the wrapper, pressing the edges together. Continue until all the filling is used up.

5 Steam the dumplings over boiling water for 5–6 minutes and then serve, garnished with the crispy fried shallots and cucumber sticks, and with the dipping sauce.

wok tip
If you don't have a steamer, these dumplings can also be gently boiled in a little water for 5–6 minutes.

Sweet-and-sour Red-cooked Fish

Preparation time: 15 minutes
Cooking time: 15 minutes

Serves 4

1 kg (2 lb) whole fish
1 teaspoon salt
2 tablespoons plain flour
vegetable oil, for deep-frying
15 g (½ oz, ⅓ cup) dried shiitake mushrooms, soaked
   in warm water for 20 minutes
50 g (2 oz, ⅓ cup) bamboo shoots, diced
3 garlic cloves, crushed
4 spring onions, chopped
3 slices fresh root ginger, peeled and shredded
25 g (1 oz, ¼ cup) water chestnuts, sliced

SAUCE:
1 tablespoon cornflour
2 tablespoons light soy sauce
2 tablespoons rice wine or dry sherry
1 tablespoon brown sugar
1 tablespoon vinegar
1 tablespoon tomato purée
2 tablespoons Fish Stock (see page 154)

1 Wash the fish and dry with kitchen paper. Use a sharp knife to slash both sides of the fish diagonally at 1.5 cm (¾ inch) intervals. Sprinkle with the salt and dredge with flour.

2 Heat the oil for deep-frying in a wok to 180–190°C (350–375°F), or until a cube of bread browns in 30 seconds. Deep-fry the whole fish for 6–8 minutes, until cooked and crisp, turning the fish half way through cooking. Remove, drain on kitchen paper and keep warm.

3 Pour off all but 3 tablespoons of oil from the wok and heat again. Drain the mushrooms, squeeze dry and discard the stems. Add to the wok with the bamboo shoots, garlic, spring onions, ginger and water chestnuts and stir-fry briskly for 3 minutes.

4 Mix together all the sauce ingredients in a bowl and stir into the wok. Keep stirring over a moderate heat until the sauce has thickened. Place the fish on a serving dish and pour the sauce over it.

wok tip
Use a whole fish such as carp, bream or mullet for this dish.

Fish with Black Bean Sauce

Preparation time: 15 minutes
Cooking time: 25–30 minutes

Serves 4

2 teaspoons sesame oil
25 g (1 oz, ¼ cup) fresh root ginger, peeled and cut
    into thin strips
1 large garlic clove, chopped
3 tablespoons fermented black beans
1 tablespoon lemon juice
2 tablespoons soy sauce
2 teaspoons sugar
150 ml (½ pint, ⅔ cup) rice wine or dry sherry
750 g (1½ lb) thick white fish fillets, in 2 pieces,
    skinned
4 large spring onions, thinly sliced diagonally, plus
    extra to garnish
1 red pepper, cored, deseeded, grilled and cut into thin
    strips, to garnish
rice noodles, to serve (optional)

1 Heat the sesame oil in a wok and add the ginger, garlic and black beans. Stir-fry for 2 minutes, then stir in the lemon juice, soy sauce, sugar and rice wine or sherry.

2 Lay the fish fillets in the sauce in the wok. Simmer gently for 20–25 minutes, until the fish is cooked through. Sprinkle the spring onions over the top of the fish, cook for just a few minutes longer, then transfer the fish and sauce to a warm serving dish. Serve immediately with rice noodles, if using, and garnished with the red pepper strips and spring onions.

wok tip
Use cod, haddock or coley for this dish. For a special occasion, use a whole sea bass instead, but make sure it is cooked through to the bone before serving.

Scallop and Prawn Stir-fry with Mixed Vegetables

Preparation time: 20–25 minutes
Cooking time: 6–8 minutes

Serves 4–6

4–6 large fresh scallops, shelled
125–175 g (4–6 oz) raw prawns, peeled and deveined
1 egg white
1 tablespoon cornflour
vegetable oil, for deep-frying
2 slices fresh root ginger, peeled and finely chopped
2–3 spring onions, sliced
3 celery sticks, trimmed and diced
1 red pepper, cored, deseeded and diced
1–2 carrots, finely diced
2 tablespoons rice wine or dry sherry
1 tablespoon light soy sauce
2 teaspoons chilli bean paste (optional)
1 teaspoon sesame oil
salt

1 Cut each scallop into 3–4 pieces. Leave the prawns whole if small, otherwise cut each one into 2 or 3 pieces. Put the seafood in a bowl with the egg white and about half of the cornflour and mix together.

2 Heat the oil in a wok, then deep-fry the scallops and prawns for 1 minute, stirring constantly with chopsticks to keep the pieces separate. Scoop them out with a slotted spoon and drain on kitchen paper.

3 Pour off all but 2 tablespoons of oil from the wok. Increase the heat to high and add the ginger and spring onions. Add the vegetables and stir-fry for about 1 minute, then return the scallops and prawns to the wok and stir in the rice wine or sherry, soy sauce and chilli bean paste, if using, and season with salt.

4 Mix the remaining cornflour to a smooth paste with a little water, then add to the wok and blend all the ingredients until thickened. Sprinkle over the sesame oil and serve immediately.

wok tip
Other vegetables work just as well with the scallops and prawns. Try sugar snap peas, mangetout or sliced baby sweetcorn instead.

Stir-fried Chicken with Shiitake Mushrooms

Preparation time: 15 minutes, plus soaking
Cooking time: 30 minutes

Serves 4

25 g (1 oz, ⅔ cup) dried shiitake mushrooms
5 tablespoons sunflower oil
2 garlic cloves, crushed
250 g (8 oz) boneless, skinless chicken breast, cut into
   strips
50 g (2 oz) baby sweetcorn cobs, blanched
175 ml (6 fl oz, ¾ cup) Chicken Stock (see page 154)
1 tablespoon Thai fish sauce
generous pinch of salt
generous pinch of sugar
½ tablespoon cornflour
2 tablespoons water

1 Soak the dried mushrooms in warm water for 20 minutes. Drain, discard the stems and cut the caps into quarters.

2 Heat the oil in a wok. Add the garlic and cook over moderate heat until golden. Add the chicken and stir-fry for 10 minutes. Lift out and set aside.

3 Add the mushrooms and sweetcorn to the oil remaining in the wok. Stir-fry for 1–2 minutes. Stir in the chicken stock and bring to the boil. Reduce the heat, return the chicken to the wok and season with fish sauce, salt and sugar.

4 Simmer for 10 minutes, or until the chicken is tender and the liquid is reduced by about half. Mix the cornflour with the water to a thin paste. Add to the chicken mixture and cook, stirring constantly, until the sauce thickens. Serve immediately.

wok tip
For a richer dish, substitute duck breast for the chicken, following the recipe in exactly the same way.

Burmese Chicken Curry with Cellophane Noodles

Preparation time: 30 minutes
Cooking time: 50 minutes

Serves 4

4 tablespoons groundnut oil
625 g (1¼ lb) boneless, skinless chicken breast, cut into bite-sized
   pieces
1½ teaspoons chilli powder
½ teaspoon ground turmeric
½ teaspoon salt
600 ml (1 pint, 2½ cups) Coconut Milk (see page 156)
300 ml (½ pint, 1¼ cups) Chicken Stock (see page 154)
50 g (2 oz, ¼ cup) creamed coconut, chopped
375 g (12 oz) cellophane noodles
a little sesame oil
salt

SPICE PASTE:
4 large garlic cloves, chopped
2 onions, chopped
1 large fresh red chilli, deseeded and chopped
2.5 cm (1 inch) piece of fresh root ginger, peeled and chopped
1 teaspoon shrimp paste

TO SERVE:
3 spring onions, sliced
2 tablespoons Crispy Fried Shallots (see page 157)
2 tablespoons Crispy Fried Garlic (see page 157)
2 tablespoons fresh coriander leaves
1 lemon, cut into wedges
whole dried chillies, fried (optional)

1 First make the spice paste. Place all the ingredients in a food processor or blender and process to a thick paste.

2 Heat the groundnut oil in a wok, add the spice paste and stir-fry over a low heat for 5 minutes, until softened.

3 Add the chicken pieces to the wok and stir-fry for a further 5 minutes to seal. Stir in the chilli powder, turmeric, salt, coconut milk and stock. Bring the curry to the boil, then reduce the heat and simmer very gently, stirring occasionally, for 15–20 minutes, or until the chicken pieces are tender.

4 Stir the creamed coconut into the curry and then simmer over a medium heat, stirring constantly, for 2–3 minutes, until the creamed coconut has dissolved and thickened the sauce slightly. Taste and adjust the seasoning if necessary.

5 Drop the noodles into a pan of salted boiling water. Bring the water back to the boil and cook the noodles for 3 minutes, or according to the packet instructions. Drain the noodles and stir in a little sesame oil.

6 To serve, divide the noodles among 4 deep soup bowls and ladle some chicken curry over each portion. Serve the accompaniments separately.

wok tip
This traditional Burmese dish is served with noodles. It is an ideal choice for an informal dinner party, as with its accompaniments, it is a meal in itself.

Paddyfield Pork

Preparation time: 15 minutes
Cooking time: 35 minutes

Serves 4

100 g (3½ oz, ¾ cup) palm sugar or light brown sugar
125 ml (4 fl oz, ½ cup) Thai fish sauce
4 tablespoons chopped shallots
2 garlic cloves, chopped
1 teaspoon pepper
500 g (1 lb) pork loin, thinly sliced
4 hard-boiled eggs, shelled and halved
Chinese chive flowers, to garnish
rice, to serve

1 Heat the sugar in a wok over a low heat until it is melted, stirring constantly. Gradually add the fish sauce and keep stirring vigorously until it is all amalgamated.

2 Add the shallots, garlic, pepper and pork slices to the caramel, cover and simmer over a low heat for about 30 minutes, stirring occasionally.

3 To serve, arrange the sliced pork on a warmed platter with the eggs and pour over the sauce, covering the eggs as well as the pork. Garnish with Chinese chive flowers and serve with rice.

wok tip
This is a Vietnamese dish, so try using Vietnamese fish sauce for a truly authentic flavour.

Stir-fried Pork with Aubergine

Preparation time: 10 minutes, plus marinating
Cooking time: 10–15 minutes

Serves 3–4

175 g (6 oz) pork fillet, sliced
2 spring onions, finely chopped, plus extra to garnish
1 garlic clove, finely chopped
1 slice fresh root ginger, peeled and finely chopped
1 tablespoon soy sauce
1 teaspoon rice wine or dry sherry
1½ teaspoons cornflour
vegetable oil, for deep-frying
250 g (8 oz) aubergine, cut into diamond-shaped chunks
1 tablespoon chilli sauce
4 tablespoons Chicken Stock (see page 154) or water
plain boiled rice, to serve

1 Put the pork in a bowl with the spring onions, garlic, ginger, soy sauce, rice wine or sherry and cornflour. Mix well, then leave to marinate for about 20 minutes.

2 Heat the oil in a wok to 180–190°C (350–375°F), or until a cube of bread browns in 30 seconds. Lower the heat, add the aubergine and deep-fry for about 1½ minutes. Remove from the pan with a slotted spoon and drain on kitchen paper.

3 Pour off all but 1 tablespoon of oil from the wok, then add the pork and stir-fry for about 1 minute.

4 Add the aubergine and chilli sauce and cook for about 1½ minutes, then moisten with the stock or water. Simmer until the liquid has almost completely evaporated. Serve hot, with plain boiled rice, garnished with chopped spring onions.

wok tip
This dish is just as successful with chicken. Follow the recipe in exactly the same way, substituting boneless, skinless chicken breast for the pork fillet.

Duck with Pineapple

Preparation time: 20 minutes
Cooking time: 1 hour 10 minutes

Serves 4

2 kg (4 lb) duck
1.2 litres (2 pints, 5 cups) water
3 tablespoons dark soy sauce
1 pineapple
a little sesame oil
2 fresh green chillies, deseeded and thinly
   sliced
1 large garlic clove
250 g (8 oz) can water chestnuts, drained and sliced
1 bunch of spring onions, sliced diagonally

1 Cut the duck in half lengthways, using a
meat cleaver and poultry scissors. Place the
halves in a wok and pour in the measured
water, then add 1 tablespoon of the soy sauce.
Put the lid on the wok and bring to the boil.
Reduce the heat so that the liquid simmers
steadily and cook for 1 hour.

2 While the duck is cooking, prepare the
pineapple: trim the leaves off the top and cut
off the stalk end. Cut off the peel and cut out
all the spines, then slice the fruit in half
lengthways and remove the hard core. Cut the
pineapple halves into slices and set them
aside.

3 Remove the duck from its stock and set
aside. Pour the stock out of the wok (chill and
skim off the fat to use the stock for Chinese
soups and stews). Wipe out the wok and oil it
with a little sesame oil.

wok tip
The combination of
simmering and frying makes the
duck meat both tender and well
flavoured. Canned pineapple in
natural juice can be used instead of
fresh but this will create a
less intense flavour.

4 When the duck is cool enough to handle,
cut all the meat off the bones and cut it into
pieces. Heat the wok and add the chillies.
Crush the garlic into the wok and add the
duck. Stir-fry until lightly browned, then add
the water chestnuts and pineapple and cook
for 1–2 minutes. Stir in the remaining soy
sauce and any juice from the fruit and sprinkle
with the spring onions. Cook for 1 minute and
serve immediately.

Beef in Oyster Sauce

Preparation time: 15 minutes, plus marinating
Cooking time: 5 minutes

Serves 4

2 tablespoons oyster sauce
1 tablespoon rice wine or dry sherry
1 tablespoon cornflour
250 g (8 oz) steak, thickly sliced
125 g (4 oz, 2 cups) dried shiitake mushrooms, soaked
   in warm water for 20 minutes
4 tablespoons vegetable oil
2 slices fresh root ginger, peeled and chopped
2 spring onions, chopped
175 g (6 oz) broccoli, divided into small florets
125 g (4 oz) bamboo shoots, sliced
1 carrot, sliced
1 teaspoon salt
1 teaspoon sugar
1 teaspoon vinegar

1 Mix together the oyster sauce, rice wine or sherry and cornflour in a bowl. Add the steak slices, turn to coat, cover and leave to marinate in the refrigerator for about 20 minutes.

2 Drain the mushrooms and squeeze dry, discard the stalks and thinly slice the caps.

3 Heat half the oil in a wok. Add the steak and stir-fry for 10–15 seconds. Remove with a slotted spoon and set aside.

4 Heat the remaining oil, then add the ginger and spring onions, mushrooms, broccoli, bamboo shoots and carrot. Add the salt and sugar and stir-fry for 1½ minutes. Add the steak, stir well and moisten with the vinegar and a little water. Heat through and serve immediately.

wok tip
Aim to make the broccoli florets an even size so that they are all cooked at the same time. Cut the carrot, too, into even slices.

Mixed Vegetables with Lemon Grass

Preparation time: 20 minutes, plus soaking
Cooking time: 15 minutes

Serves 4

vegetable oil, for frying
125 g (4 oz) firm tofu, cut into 1 cm (½ inch) cubes
3 lemon grass stalks, finely chopped
2 large garlic cloves, finely chopped
1 leek, white part only, thinly sliced
250 g (8 oz) Chinese leaves, thinly sliced
3 dried shiitake mushrooms, soaked in warm water for
    20 minutes and sliced
60 g (2½ oz, 1 cup) oyster mushrooms, torn
125 g (4 oz) mangetout
1 bunch of watercress
6 baby sweetcorn cobs
1 long mild red chilli, deseeded and thinly sliced
100 ml (3½ fl oz, ½ cup) Vegetable Stock (page 154)
1 tablespoon light soy sauce
1 teaspoon palm sugar or light brown sugar
1 tablespoon dark soy sauce
salt and pepper

1 Heat about 1 cm (½ inch) of oil in a wok and add the tofu. Cook until golden on all sides then remove and drain on kitchen paper.

2 Drain all but 1 tablespoon of the oil from the wok and reheat it. Add the lemon grass, garlic and leek and stir-fry for about 1 minute, then add the remaining vegetables, a few at a time, stirring constantly. Add the stock, light soy sauce, sugar and dark soy sauce, stir and cover. Cook over a moderate heat for about 6 minutes, stirring occasionally. Stir in the tofu, season with salt and pepper and serve hot.

wok tip
This Vietnamese dish makes a lovely main course if it is served with steamed jasmine rice.

White Cabbage Salad

Preparation time: 20 minutes
Cooking time: 10–15 minutes

Serves 4

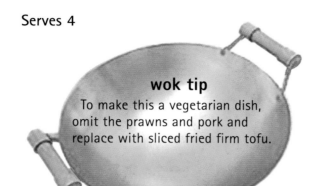

wok tip
To make this a vegetarian dish, omit the prawns and pork and replace with sliced fried firm tofu.

300 g (10 oz, 3 cups) white cabbage, thinly sliced
3 tablespoons vegetable oil
1 tablespoon sliced shallots
1 garlic clove, crushed
1 tablespoon chopped dried red chillies
1 tablespoon Thai fish sauce
1½ tablespoons lemon juice
1 tablespoon Crushed Roasted Peanuts (see page 157)
4 tablespoons Coconut Cream (see page 156)
10 cooked king prawns, peeled, deveined and halved lengthways
250 g (8 oz) sliced roast pork
salt

1 Add the cabbage to a saucepan of boiling water and cook over a high heat for 2 minutes. Drain the cabbage in a colander, refresh it under cold running water, return it to the pan and heat through.

2 Heat the oil in a wok. Add the shallots and stir-fry for 2 minutes, then transfer with a slotted spoon to kitchen paper to drain. Add the garlic to the oil remaining in the wok and stir-fry over a gentle heat until just golden. Drain on kitchen paper. Add more oil to the wok if necessary, then add the red chillies and stir-fry for 2 minutes. Drain on kitchen paper.

3 Transfer the cabbage to a large bowl, add the fish sauce, lemon juice, peanuts, coconut cream, prawns, sliced pork and salt to taste, then mix well. Spoon the salad on to a warm serving plate, sprinkle with the stir-fried shallots, garlic and chillies, and serve immediately.

Spicy Fried Rice with Red Chillies

Preparation time: 15 minutes
Cooking time: 25–35 minutes

Serves 4

375 g (12 oz, 2¼ cups) long-grain rice
750 ml (1¼ pints, 3 cups) water
2 tablespoons sunflower oil
4 shallots or 1 onion, thinly sliced
2 fresh red chillies, deseeded and thinly sliced
50 g (2 oz) lean boneless pork, beef or bacon, finely
   diced
1 tablespoon light soy sauce
1 teaspoon tomato purée
salt

TO GARNISH:
fried onion rings
omelette strips
fresh coriander leaves
cucumber slices

1 Rinse the rice in a sieve under cold running water and drain well. Place the rice in a saucepan, pour in the measured water, and add a pinch of salt. Bring to the boil, stir once, cover and simmer for 15–20 minutes, or until the water has been absorbed. Remove from the heat and set aside in the covered pan.

2 Heat the oil in a wok, add the shallots or onion and chillies and stir-fry for 1–3 minutes. Add the meat and stir-fry for 3 minutes.

3 Add the rice, soy sauce and tomato purée. Stir-fry for 5–8 minutes, then season with salt to taste.

4 Transfer the rice mixture to a warmed serving dish or bowls. Garnish with fried onion rings, strips of omelette, coriander leaves and cucumber slices. Serve immediately.

wok tip
To make the omelette strips, beat one egg in a dish and season lightly. Heat a little oil in a wok, pour in the egg and swirl around the wok to form a thin omelette. When it has set, put it on a plate, roll it up and cut into strips.

New Potato Curry

Preparation time: 10 minutes
Cooking time: 20–25 minutes

Serves 4

25 g (1 oz, 2 tablespoons) butter
1 tablespoon vegetable oil
2 large onions, finely chopped
50 g (2 oz, ½ cup) fresh root ginger, peeled and grated
2 garlic cloves, crushed
2 bay leaves
1 cinnamon stick, broken in half
2 teaspoons fennel seeds
3 green cardamoms
1 teaspoon ground turmeric
1 kg (2 lb) small new potatoes
600 ml (1 pint, 2½ cups) water
300 ml (½ pint, 1¼ cups) natural yogurt
chilli powder, to taste
salt and pepper

TO GARNISH:
chopped fresh coriander
4 kaffir lime leaves

wok tip
Serve this curry as a main course, accompanied either by a dish of peeled prawns, sprinkled with grated lemon rind and chilli powder, or quartered hard-boiled eggs sprinkled with paprika, chopped thyme and salt and pepper.

1 Heat the butter and oil in a wok. Add the onions, ginger, garlic, bay leaves, cinnamon, fennel seeds, cardamoms and turmeric. Stir-fry until the onion is softened, but not browned.

2 Stir in the potatoes, pour in the measured water and add salt and pepper to taste. Bring to the boil and cover the wok. Simmer for 10 minutes, then uncover and cook fairly rapidly for a further 10 minutes, or until most of the water has evaporated.

3 Pour the yogurt over the potatoes and heat gently to avoid curdling the sauce. Sprinkle with chilli powder to taste before garnishing the curry with chopped coriander and kaffir lime leaves.

Egg-fried Noodles with Vegetables and Tofu

Preparation time: 20 minutes
Cooking time: 15–18 minutes

Serves 4

vegetable oil, for deep-frying
250 g (8 oz) firm tofu, cubed
125 g (4 oz) broccoli florets
125 g (4 oz) baby sweetcorn cobs, halved
3 tablespoons light soy sauce
1 tablespoon lemon juice
1 teaspoon sugar
1 teaspoon chilli sauce
3 tablespoons sunflower oil
1 garlic clove, chopped
1 red chilli, deseeded and sliced
75 g (3 oz) dried thread egg noodles, cooked
2 eggs, lightly beaten
125 g (4 oz, 1 cup) water chestnuts, sliced

1 Heat about 5 cm (2 inches) of vegetable oil in a wok to 180–190°C (350–375°F), or until a cube of bread browns in 30 seconds. Add the tofu and fry for 3–4 minutes, until crisp and lightly golden. Drain the tofu on kitchen paper.

2 Blanch the broccoli and sweetcorn in a saucepan of boiling water for 1 minute, then drain, refresh under cold water and pat dry with kitchen paper. In a bowl, mix together the soy sauce, lemon juice, sugar and chilli sauce and set aside.

3 Heat the sunflower oil in a wok, add the garlic and chilli and stir-fry for 3 minutes. Add the noodles and stir-fry for 5 minutes, until golden and starting to crisp up.

4 Stir in the eggs, and stir-fry for 1 minute, then stir in the soy sauce mixture, tofu, vegetables and water chestnuts and cook for a further 2–3 minutes, until heated through. Serve immediately.

wok tip
Cook the noodles according to the packet instructions, drain, refresh under cold water and dry well on kitchen paper before adding to the wok.

Noodles with Chicken and Prawns

wok tip
To vary this simple dish, try adding shiitake mushrooms with the broccoli. A garnish of pieces of shredded cooked ham also makes a tasty addition.

Preparation time: 10 minutes
Cooking time: 20 minutes

Serves 6

4 tablespoons vegetable oil
2 garlic cloves, crushed
125 g (4 oz) fresh thread egg noodles
2 tablespoons dark soy sauce
125 g (4 oz) mixed raw sliced chicken breast, prepared squid and shelled prawns
½ teaspoon pepper
2 tablespoons Thai fish sauce
125 g (4 oz) mixed shredded cabbage and broccoli florets
300 ml (½ pint, 1¼ cups) Chicken Stock (see page 154)
1 tablespoon cornflour
2 tablespoons sugar

1 Heat half the oil in a wok. Add half the garlic and stir-fry for 1 minute until golden brown. Add the noodles and 1 tablespoon of soy sauce and cook, stirring constantly for 3–5 minutes. Transfer to a serving dish and keep warm.

2 Heat the remaining oil in the wok and add the rest of the garlic. Stir-fry for 1 minute until golden brown. Add the chicken breast, squid, prawns, pepper and the fish sauce. Stir-fry for 5 minutes.

3 Add the shredded cabbage and broccoli florets to the meat mixture in the wok, and stir-fry for 3 minutes.

4 Stir in the stock. Mix the cornflour with 2 tablespoons of water and stir into the wok. Add the remaining soy sauce and sugar, and bring to the boil. Lower the heat and cook for 3 minutes, stirring constantly. Pour the sauce over the noodles and serve immediately.

Viva Vegetarian

In Asia, the origins of not eating meat can be traced back to ancient eastern religions like Hinduism and Buddhism, and to economic constraints which resulted in the development of a cuisine that relied heavily on vegetables and made a little meat go a long way. With its focus on rice and noodles, vegetables, tofu, nuts and fruit, it is a style of cooking already geared towards Western vegetarians. Add to this the modern trend for enhancing the role of vegetables as main dish ingredients rather than side dish accompaniments and the increased availability of manufactured vegetable proteins like tofu and TVP (see below) and their suitability for wok cookery and you have the perfect cuisine for today's vegetarians.

Importance of soya

Soya is invaluable to vegetarians, being an excellent source of non-animal protein and other nutrients. Rarely used as a bean in its own right, soya is more commonly used in other forms such as tofu, tempeh, miso and soy sauce, all of which are widely used in Oriental cooking.

Tofu, or soya bean curd, is a versatile product made from curdled soya milk, which has been extracted from soya beans. The tofu's texture depends on how much liquid has been removed. Available plain, preserved, smoked or marinated, firm tofu can be cubed or sliced. Virtually tasteless, plain tofu absorbs the flavours of the food with which it is cooked. It is therefore best marinated before use – ideally in stir-fries. It is low in calories, saturated

---

Vegetarian extras

In addition to the ingredients listed on pages 116 and 117, the following are useful for Asian vegetarian cooking:

- arrowroot
- curry paste
- vegetarian fish sauce
- miso
- nuts – unsalted almonds, peanuts or cashew nuts
- vegetarian oyster sauce
- sesame seeds
- shoyu
- tamari
- baby bean sprouts

---

fat and salt, and a good source of protein, B vitamins, iron and calcium.

Tempeh is another food made from fermented cooked soya beans, but has a different texture to tofu.

TVP (textured vegetable protein), often called dried soya mince, is another low-fat, high-fibre, high-protein product useful for imitating conventional meat. Available as dried chunks, mince or flakes, TVP requires the addition of water before use. Its sponge-like texture and bland taste means that this protein, too, is best marinated as it absorbs flavours well in cooking.

Miso is a savoury paste made from fermented soya beans, which is usually added at the end of cooking to

Asian-style vegetarian cooking

- Use no more than four or five types of vegetable in vegetable stir-fries – mix crisp vegetables like green beans with leafy ones like Chinese leaves.

- Improve the taste of tofu, tempeh, TVP or seitan by marinating before cooking.

- Use only crisp, firm vegetables for stir-frying. Cut them just before cooking to preserve their vitamins or prepare in advance and store refrigerated in a sealed container.

- Be aware that many seemingly vegetarian dishes may use fish sauce or shrimp paste. Replace fish sauce with soy sauce, vegetarian fish sauce or vegetarian oyster sauce. Use light miso instead of shrimp paste.

- Cut stir-fry vegetables diagonally or into thin strips to increase the surface area that comes into contact with the oil. This ensures fast cooking and preserves their texture, flavour, colour and nutritional content.

- Briefly blanch denser vegetables like aubergine, broccoli and cauliflower florets, green beans or thickly cut carrots before stir-frying if preferred. Alternatively, simply add the harder vegetables to the wok first and cook for a few minutes before adding softer ones.

- Use shredded spring onions or leeks in stir-fries rather than ordinary onions for their milder flavour and softer texture.

- Remember that leafy vegetables like pak choi reduce greatly in volume when cooked so start with plenty of greens.

- If you are using dried mushrooms, rehydrate them in warm water and use the soaking liquid as required in a recipe instead of water.

- Add water chestnuts to vegetarian stir-fries for both texture and sweetness, or add mung bean sprouts if you only want the crunch.

preserve its live bacteria. Check the label when buying miso as some Japanese brands contain fish stock.

Tamari, **shoyu** and **soy sauce** are Oriental sauces with a strong, salty taste, all fermented from soya beans.

Other vegetable proteins

Seitan, also known as wheat meat, is derived from wheat gluten. It is another low-fat, protein-rich meat substitute that absorbs the flavours of other foods and works well in stir-fries and other Asian-style vegetarian recipes.

Beans, peas, nuts and seeds are other vegetarian sources of protein that are widely used in wok cookery. Be wary of eating too many nuts and seeds (no more than a handful a day) because of their high fat content.

chapter 5
Spiced for Life

A range of exciting dishes from all over Asia that are guaranteed to stimulate your taste buds. There is also a feature on key ingredients, such as marinades, sauces, pastes and oils, and how to use them to maximize flavour.

Sole with Herbs and Satay Sauce

Preparation time: 35 minutes
Cooking time: 15–20 minutes

Serves 4
25 g (1 oz, 2 tablespoons) butter
1 shallot, finely chopped
1 tablespoon each chopped fresh chives, tarragon and
    parsley
grated rind of ½ lemon
8 sole fillets
1 egg, beaten
4–5 tablespoons fresh breadcrumbs
sunflower oil, for deep-frying
flat leaf parsley, to garnish

SATAY SAUCE:
1 teaspoon each of coriander, cumin and fennel seeds,
    crushed

2 garlic cloves, crushed
125 g (4 oz, ½ cup) crunchy peanut butter
1 teaspoon dark soft brown sugar
2 fresh green chillies, deseeded and chopped
150 g (5 oz, ⅔ cup) creamed coconut
450 ml (¾ pint, 2 cups) water
3 tablespoons lemon juice

1 First make the sauce. Heat a wok, add the spice seeds and stir-fry for 2 minutes. Add the garlic, peanut butter, sugar and chillies. Combine the creamed coconut with the water and stir it into the wok. Cook gently for 7–8 minutes. Stir in the lemon juice.

2 Meanwhile, melt the butter in a pan, add the shallot and cook for 1 minute. Stir in the herbs and lemon rind. Cool slightly. Divide this mixture between the fish fillets. Roll up each one and secure with wooden cocktail sticks.

3 Dip in the egg and coat in breadcrumbs. Heat the oil in a wok to 180–190°C (350–375°F), or until a cube of bread browns in 30 seconds. Deep-fry the fish for 4–5 minutes, until golden. Drain and serve, garnish with parsley, with the sauce served separately.

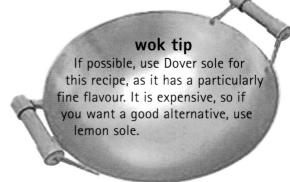

wok tip
If possible, use Dover sole for this recipe, as it has a particularly fine flavour. It is expensive, so if you want a good alternative, use lemon sole.

Spicy Fishcakes

Preparation time: 20 minutes
Cooking time: about 30 minutes

Serves 4-5

500 g (1 lb) cod fillet, skinned and cut into chunks
3 tablespoons Red Curry Paste (see page 155)
1 egg
3 tablespoons Thai fish sauce
1-2 tablespoons rice flour
75 g (3 oz, ¾ cup) thin green beans, finely chopped
1 tablespoon finely shredded kaffir lime leaves or
   ½ teaspoon grated lime rind
vegetable oil, for deep-frying

TO SERVE:
Chilli Sauce (see page 156)
lime slices
cucumber salad

1 Put the cod and red curry paste in a food processor or blender. Process to a paste. Alternatively, pound the fish and curry paste in a mortar with a pestle.

2 Transfer the fish to a bowl. Add the egg, fish sauce, and sufficient rice flour to knead with your hands into a stiff mixture. Work in the beans and lime leaves or lime rind.

3 Form the fish mixture into 16-20 balls and, using your hands, flatten each ball into a round, about 1 cm (½ inch) thick.

4 Heat the oil in a wok and fry the fishcakes, a few at a time, for 4-5 minutes on each side, until they are cooked and golden. Take care not to overcook them. Drain on kitchen paper and serve hot with chilli sauce, slices of lime and a cucumber salad.

wok tip
These fish cakes are quite spicy. If you do not like your food too hot, reduce the amount of chillies in the curry paste or reduce the amount of curry paste you use.

Fish in Tamarind Sauce

Preparation time: 15 minutes
Cooking time: 10–15 minutes

Serves 4

1 John Dory or lemon sole, filleted
vegetable oil, for deep-frying
¼ head of white cabbage, shredded, to serve

TAMARIND SAUCE:
3 tablespoons vegetable oil
2–3 garlic cloves, crushed
1–2 fresh red or green chillies, deseeded and finely chopped
125 ml (4 fl oz, ½ cup) Tamarind Water (see page 156)
1 tablespoon Thai fish sauce
3 tablespoons soft brown sugar

TO GARNISH:
2 tablespoons chopped fresh coriander leaves
1 red pepper, cored, deseeded and chopped
1 green pepper, cored, deseeded and chopped

1 Pat the fish dry with kitchen paper. Heat the oil for deep-frying in the wok to 180–190°C (350–375°F), or until a cube of bread browns in 30 seconds. Deep-fry the fish fillets for 10–15 minutes, until golden brown. Using a slotted spoon, carefully remove the fish from the oil and drain it on kitchen paper. Transfer the fish to a serving dish and keep hot.

2 Meanwhile, make the sauce. Heat the vegetable oil in a small saucepan, add the garlic and chilli and stir-fry for about 2 minutes, until golden, but not brown. Stir in the tamarind water, fish sauce and brown sugar and bring to the boil. Cook for a further 3 minutes, stirring constantly.

3 Pour the sauce over the fish. Garnish with chopped coriander and chopped peppers. Serve immediately with a salad of shredded cabbage.

wok tip
The tamarind sauce adds a sweet-and-sour flavour to this dish, which contrasts well with the fried fish. As an alternative, use scallops or prawns instead of the fish, adjusting the cooking time accordingly.

King Prawn and Coconut Curry

Preparation time: 10 minutes
Cooking time: 15 minutes

Serves 4

2 tablespoons groundnut oil
1 teaspoon ground turmeric
150 ml (¼ pint, ⅔ cup) water
150 ml (¼ pint, ⅔ cup) Coconut Milk (see page 156)
2 tablespoons lime juice
2 teaspoons soft brown sugar
16 raw king prawns, peeled and deveined
salt and pepper

SPICE PASTE:
2 fresh red chillies, deseeded and chopped
2 shallots, chopped
1 lemon grass stalk, chopped
2.5 cm (1 inch) piece of fresh root ginger, peeled and chopped
½ teaspoon shrimp paste (optional)

TO GARNISH:
4 spring onions, sliced into thin strips
thin slices of coconut
1 tablespoon desiccated coconut

1 Place all the ingredients for the spice paste in a blender or spice mill and blend to produce a thick paste. Alternatively, pound the ingredients in a mortar with a pestle.

2 Heat the oil in a wok, add the paste and turmeric and then cook over a gentle heat, stirring frequently, for 3 minutes.

3 Add the measured water to the wok, mix well and simmer gently for 3 minutes. Stir in the coconut milk, lime juice and sugar and simmer for a further 3 minutes.

4 Add the prawns to the curry and cook for 4–5 minutes, until they turn pink and are cooked through. Season to taste.

5 Transfer the curry to a warm serving dish and serve immediately, garnished with spring onions, coconut slices and desiccated coconut.

wok tip
This dish can also be garnished with Crispy Fried Shallots (see page 157) or Crushed Roasted Peanuts (see page 157) for a richer taste.

Braised Aubergines

Preparation time: 15 minutes
Cooking time: 7–10 minutes

Serves 4–6

vegetable oil, for frying
4 spring onions, sliced
4 garlic cloves, sliced
2.5 cm (1 inch) piece of fresh root ginger, peeled and
   finely sliced
2 large aubergines, cut into 5 cm (2 inch) strips
2 tablespoons soy sauce
2 tablespoons rice wine or dry sherry
2 teaspoons chilli sauce

TO GARNISH:
1 fresh red chilli, deseeded and chopped
1 fresh green chilli, deseeded and chopped

1 Heat 2 tablespoons of oil in a wok. Add the spring onions, garlic and ginger and stir-fry for about 30 seconds. Remove the mixture from the wok and set aside.

2 Increase the heat, add the aubergines and stir-fry until they are browned, adding more oil as necessary. Using a slotted spoon, remove the aubergines and drain on kitchen paper.

3 Pour off the oil from the wok. Return the spring onions, garlic, ginger and aubergine to the wok and add the soy sauce, rice wine or sherry and chilli sauce. Stir well and cook for 2 minutes.

4 Spoon the aubergines into a warm serving dish, garnish with red and green chillies and serve immediately.

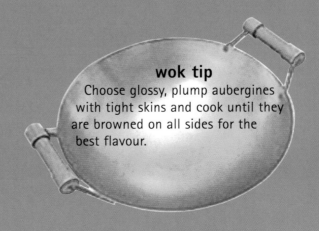

wok tip
Choose glossy, plump aubergines with tight skins and cook until they are browned on all sides for the best flavour.

Chicken with Chilli and Black Bean Sauce

Preparation time: 10–15 minutes
Cooking time: about 20 minutes

Serves 2–4

1 egg white
1 tablespoon cornflour
2 boneless, skinless chicken breasts, cut into thin strips across the
    grain
about 300 ml (½ pint, 1¼ cups) groundnut oil
1 green pepper, cored, deseeded and cut lengthways into thin
    strips
1 fresh green chilli, deseeded and very finely shredded
4 garlic cloves, cut into very thin strips
4 spring onions, shredded
4 tablespoons black bean sauce
300 ml (½ pint, 1¼ cups) hot Chicken Stock (see page 154)
salt and pepper
1–2 heaped tablespoons canned fermented black beans, rinsed, to
    garnish
egg noodles, to serve

1 Put the egg white into a bowl with salt and pepper to taste and whisk with a fork until frothy. Sift in the cornflour and whisk to mix, then add the chicken and stir until coated.

2 Heat the oil in a wok until very hot, but not smoking. Add about one-quarter of the chicken strips and stir to separate. Stir-fry for 30–60 seconds, until the chicken turns white on all sides. Lift out with a slotted spoon and drain on kitchen paper. Repeat with the remaining chicken. Very carefully pour off all but about 1 tablespoon of the hot oil from the wok.

3 Return the wok to a low heat and add the green pepper, chilli, garlic and about half of the spring onions.

wok tip

The technique of coating and frying the chicken at the beginning is called 'velveting' and is used to protect the delicate flesh. The chicken has a perfect finish – slightly crisp on the outside and meltingly tender inside.

Stir-fry for a few minutes, until the pepper begins to soften, then add the black bean sauce and stir to mix. Pour in the stock, increase the heat to high and bring to the boil, stirring constantly.

4 Put the chicken into the sauce and cook over a moderate to high heat, stirring frequently, for 5 minutes. Taste for seasoning. Serve hot with egg noodles, garnished with the remaining spring onions and the black beans.

Goan Chicken Shakuti

Preparation time: 20 minutes
Cooking time: 1 hour

Serves 4

3 dried Kashmiri chillies
2 teaspoons ground cumin
1 tablespoon coriander seeds
1 teaspoon fenugreek seeds
½ teaspoon peppercorns
½ teaspoon cloves
seeds from 4 cardamom pods
1 small cinnamon stick
1 teaspoon ground turmeric
3 tablespoons vegetable oil
2 onions, finely chopped
3 garlic cloves, crushed
50 g (2 oz, ¾ cup) desiccated coconut, toasted
1.5 kg (3 lb) chicken, jointed
25 g (1 oz, ¼ cup) roasted peanuts, roughly chopped
150 ml (¼ pint, ⅔ cup) Coconut Milk (see page 156)
150 ml (¼ pint, ⅔ cup) Chicken Stock (see page 157)
8 tablespoons lemon juice
½ teaspoon salt

wok tip
Shakuti is a Goanese speciality; it is rich and full of the flavour of coconut. To toast the coconut, heat a wok or frying pan until hot and dry-fry the coconut, until it is golden.

1 Spread the chillies, cumin, coriander seeds, fenugreek seeds, peppercorns and cloves on a baking sheet and roast in a preheated oven, 200°C (400°F), Gas Mark 6, for 5 minutes. Allow to cool slightly, then grind to a powder with the cardamom seeds and cinnamon. Add the turmeric.

2 Heat the oil in a wok and fry the onions and garlic until softened and beginning to brown. Add the spice mixture and toasted coconut and fry, stirring constantly, for 1 minute.

3 Add the chicken to the wok and seal in the oil. Add the peanuts, coconut milk and stock and simmer gently for 40 minutes.

4 Once the chicken has cooked through and is tender, add the lemon juice and salt. Simmer for a further 5 minutes, then serve.

Chicken and Lemon Grass Curry

Preparation time: 20 minutes
Cooking time: 10–15 minutes

Serves 4

2 tablespoons groundnut oil
2 garlic cloves, finely chopped
3 shallots, thinly sliced
3 lemon grass stalks, crushed and cut into 2.5 cm
   (1 inch) pieces
2 tablespoons Thai fish sauce
½ teaspoon pepper
½ teaspoon palm sugar or light brown sugar
1 teaspoon Yellow Curry Paste (see page 155) or
   korma curry paste
2 small fresh green chillies, deseeded and chopped
750 g (1½ lb) boneless, skinless chicken breast, cut
   into thin strips
3 tablespoons Chicken Stock (see page 154)
125 ml (4 fl oz, ½ cup) Coconut Milk (see page 156)

TO GARNISH:
2 tablespoons Crushed Roasted Peanuts (see page 157)
handful of fresh coriander leaves

1 Heat the oil in a wok, add the garlic and shallots and stir-fry for 1 minute. Add the lemon grass, fish sauce, pepper, sugar, curry paste, chillies and chicken strips and stir-fry for 3–4 minutes.

2 Add the stock and coconut milk, mix well and simmer gently for 6 minutes, or until the chicken is cooked through. Serve garnished with peanuts and coriander leaves.

wok tip
To make Prawn and Lemon Grass Curry, omit the chicken, but add 16–20 raw tiger or king prawns with the stock and coconut milk. If you prefer, swap the chicken stock for fish stock (see page 154).

Red Curry Duck

Preparation time: 15 minutes
Cooking time: 5 minutes

Serves 3–4

¼ cold cooked duck, or 1 cooked duck breast
1 tablespoon oil
1½ tablespoons Red Curry Paste (see page 155)
75 ml (3 fl oz, 4½ tablespoons) Coconut Milk
   (see page 156)
1 tablespoon palm sugar or light brown sugar
3 kaffir lime leaves, torn
50 g (2 oz, ½ cup) fresh or frozen peas
1 large fresh red chilli, deseeded and sliced diagonally
4 tablespoons Chicken Stock (see page 154)
2 tomatoes, finely diced
75 g (3 oz) fresh or canned pineapple, cut into
   chunks, plus extra to serve
1 tablespoon Thai fish sauce
noodles, to serve

TO GARNISH:
red pepper strips
spring onion strips

1 Take the skin and meat off the duck, chop
the flesh into bite-sized pieces and set aside.

wok tip
This recipe is a great way
to use up any cold cooked duck.
Other cold cooked meats could also
be used instead, such as chicken,
turkey and pork.

2 Heat the oil in a wok, add the curry paste
and stir-fry for 30 seconds. Add 3 tablespoons
of the coconut milk, mix it with the paste,
then add the remainder and stir over a gentle
heat for 1 minute.

3 Add the duck and stir for 2 minutes. Add
the sugar, lime leaves, peas, chilli, chicken
stock, tomatoes and pineapple. Mix
thoroughly, then when the curry is simmering,
add the fish sauce. Stir well and transfer to a
bowl. Serve with extra pineapple and noodles,
garnished with red pepper and green onion
strips.

Lamb with Spicy Hot Sauce

Preparation time: 10 minutes, plus freezing and thawing
Cooking time: about 10 minutes

Serves 3–4

500 g (1 lb) lamb neck fillet
3 tablespoons groundnut oil
4 spring onions, thinly sliced diagonally
2 garlic cloves, crushed
6–8 small fresh chillies, to garnish (optional)
cellophane noodles, to serve

SAUCE:
2 teaspoons cornflour
4 tablespoons water
1–2 tablespoons hot chilli sauce
1 tablespoon rice wine vinegar or white wine or cider
   vinegar
2 teaspoons dark soft brown sugar
½ teaspoon Chinese five-spice powder

wok tip
Take care – this simple
stir-fry is fiery hot. Different brands
of chilli sauce vary in their spiciness.
Adjust the quantity used to suit
your brand and your taste.

1 Wrap the lamb in clingfilm and place it in the freezer for 1–2 hours, until it is just hard. Cut it into thin strips across the grain, discarding any fat and sinew. Leave at room temperature for about 30 minutes, or until the meat has completely thawed.

2 To prepare the sauce, blend the cornflour to a thin paste with the measured water, then stir in the chilli sauce, vinegar, sugar and five-spice powder.

3 Heat 2 tablespoons of the oil in a wok. Add the lamb and stir-fry over a high heat for 3–4 minutes, or until browned on all sides. Remove the wok from the heat and tip the lamb and its juices into a bowl.

4 Return the wok to a moderate heat. Add the remaining oil and heat until hot. Add the spring onions and garlic and stir-fry for 30 seconds. Remove with a slotted spoon.

5 Stir the sauce to mix, pour into the pan and increase the heat to high. Stir until the sauce thickens, then add the lamb and its juices and the spring onion mixture. Toss for 1–2 minutes, or until piping hot. Serve immediately, with cellophane noodles. Garnish with a few small chillies, if liked.

Green Bean Sambal

Preparation time: 15 minutes
Cooking time: 15 minutes

Serves 4

2 tablespoons vegetable oil
4 shallots, thinly sliced
2 garlic cloves, crushed
½ teaspoon shrimp paste
250 g (8 oz) French beans, trimmed and thinly sliced
    diagonally
2 teaspoons sambal oelek
1 teaspoon soft brown sugar
salt

1 Heat the oil in a wok, add the shallots, garlic and shrimp paste and fry over a low heat, stirring frequently, for 5 minutes, until the shallots are softened.

2 Add the beans, increase the heat to moderate and fry, stirring occasionally, for 8 minutes, until the beans are cooked but not too soft.

3 Stir in the sambal oelek, sugar and a little salt and continue frying the beans for a further 1 minute. Taste and add a little more salt if necessary. Serve the sambal hot.

wok tip
Sambal oelek is a hot pepper condiment, available in Asian supermarkets.

Sayur Kari

Preparation time: 15 minutes
Cooking time: about 30 minutes

Serves 6

2 tablespoons vegetable oil, plus extra for deep-frying
4 squares of yellow tofu, cut into 2.5 cm (1 inch) cubes
4 shallots, sliced
2 fresh green chillies, deseeded and sliced
3 garlic cloves, chopped
1 tablespoon finely chopped fresh root ginger
1 lemon grass stalk, finely chopped
1 tablespoon ground coriander
1 teaspoon ground cumin
1 teaspoon ground turmeric
1 teaspoon galangal powder (optional)
1 teaspoon chilli powder
1 teaspoon shrimp paste
600 ml (1 pint, 2½ cups) Vegetable Stock (see page 154)
400 ml (14 fl oz, 1¾ cups) Coconut Milk (see page 156)
250 g (8 oz, 1½ cups) potato, diced
125 g (4 oz) green beans, trimmed and cut into 1 cm (½ inch) lengths
125 g (4 oz, 1¼ cups) white cabbage, finely shredded
75 g (3 oz) bean sprouts
25 g (1 oz, ¼ cup) rice vermicelli, soaked in boiling water for 5 minutes and drained
salt

1 Heat the oil for deep-frying in a wok to 180–190°C (350–375°F), or until a cube of bread browns in 30 seconds. Deep-fry the tofu cubes, in batches, for about 1 minute, until they are crisp and golden. Remove with a slotted spoon, and set aside to drain on kitchen paper.

2 Drain off all but 2 tablespoons of oil from the wok and reheat. Add the shallots, chillies, garlic, ginger and lemon grass and fry over a gentle heat, stirring frequently, for 5 minutes, until softened.

3 Add the coriander, cumin, turmeric, galangal powder, chilli powder and shrimp paste. Fry the mixture for 1 minute. Stir in the stock and coconut milk. Bring to the boil and add the potato. Reduce the heat and cook the potato for 6 minutes. Add the beans and cook for a further 8 minutes.

4 Stir in the cabbage, bean sprouts and rice vermicelli, season with salt to taste and cook gently for a further 3 minutes. Stir in the fried tofu and serve.

wok tip
Sayur Kari is an Indonesian vegetable curry, best served with rice. If yellow tofu is not available, use firm-textured tofu as found in many supermarkets and wholefood shops.

Marinades and more

Black bean sauce
This rich, thick sauce is made from black soya beans. It is readily available in cans and jars or can be made at home. Simply blend sugar, garlic and soy sauce to taste, then mix with a rinsed can of fermented black beans.

Chilli bean paste
Made from soya beans and chillies, this thick paste has a rich, spicy flavour. If you can't get it, use yellow bean paste and a little chopped fresh red chilli instead.

Chilli oil
This fiery, pungent oil is used as a flavouring rather than for frying. It can be bought from Oriental stores or you can make your own by placing a few dried red chillies in groundnut oil and leaving them to steep.

Chilli sauce
Chilli sauce is a rich, red sauce with a hot, spicy taste. It is made from red chillies and is used in many different cuisines. Mostly it is sparingly incorporated into a dish, but it is generously used in Szechuan cooking, which is renowned for its spiciness. Some brands are fiery hot, while others are mild and sweet, so take care when using a brand for the first time.

Dark soy sauce
This is the best-known and most widely used flavouring. It is richer, thicker and sweeter than light soy sauce, but is made in the same way from fermented soya beans, yeast, salt and sugar. It is used in meat dishes and as a dipping sauce in its own right.

Dried black fungus
Black fungus, also known as cloud ear or wood ear, is a large curly fungus. It is most often used dried and should be soaked in warm water for 20 minutes, then rinsed and sliced before use.

Dried chillies
Dried chillies are perfect for flavouring oil for stir-frying and in spicy, hot-flavoured pastes and oils. Stored in an airtight container, they will keep for ages and maintain their red colour and fiery flavour. Use them with care, as they can be very hot.

Dried citrus peel
Dried citrus peel is sold in packets in Chinese supermarkets. It has a sharp, bittersweet tang, which is delicious in stir-fries.

Dried shiitake mushrooms
The shiitake mushroom has a golden brown cap and light gills and stem, and an intensely aromatic flavour. In China, they are often dried, making their flavour more pronounced. Dried mushrooms should be soaked in warm water for 20 minutes to rehydrate them. They can then be used like fresh mushrooms. The stems are often tough, so they should be removed and discarded.

Fermented black beans
These have a rich, salty and earthy flavour and can be bought in cans. They are moist and wrinkled and are often ground to a paste and mixed with spices to make black bean sauce.

Five-spice powder
Available in supermarkets and Oriental stores, five-spice powder is a fragrant mixture of five ground spices: star anise, cinnamon, cloves, fennel seeds and Szechuan peppercorns. It is used extensively in Chinese and Malaysian cooking and has an aromatic rather than a spicy taste.

Hoisin sauce
One of the most commonly used Chinese sauces, hoisin is available from supermarkets and Chinese stores. It is used for grilling and barbecuing and is also served separately as a dipping sauce. It is made from soya beans, tomato purée and spices.

Light soy sauce
Light soy sauce has a delicate, mildly salty flavour and is much paler in colour than dark soy. The colour of the

sauce depends on the length of time it has been aged. Light soy sauce tends to be used in seafood dishes, soups and as a dipping sauce.

Oyster sauce
This is a thick, dark brown sauce made from oysters and soy sauce. It has a rich, sweet fishy flavour and is added to stir-fried dishes, most often with beef.

Palm sugar
Palm sugar is extracted from palms and used throughout South-east Asia. It is usually sold in small round blocks, which can be crumbled for use. If it is unavailable, use light muscovado or any light brown sugar instead.

Plum sauce
Plum sauce is a sweet sauce made from plums, apricots, vinegar, garlic and seasonings and is incorporated into braised dishes or used as a dipping sauce.

Red bean paste
Sweetened red bean paste is sold in cans in Chinese supermarkets. It is a very thick paste that is a dark reddish brown in colour. Once the can has been opened, decant any leftover paste into an airtight container and keep it in the refrigerator or freezer.

Rice wine
Made from glutinous rice and yeast, rice wine is often used in Chinese cooking. Dry sherry can be used instead.

Rice wine vinegar
This is made from fermented rice wine. Red rice wine vinegar is sweeter and spicier than white. Use distilled white vinegar or cider vinegar if it is not available.

Sesame seed paste
Sesame seed paste is made from crushed sesame seeds and has an intense nutty flavour. It is available from Oriental stores and health food shops. Tahini makes a good substitute.

Shrimp paste
Available fresh or dried in plastic tubs or wrapped blocks, this is made from salted, fermented shrimp and is a major source of protein in many South-east Asian diets. The dried blocks are stronger than the fresh.

Szechuan peppercorns
Aromatic rather than hot, Szechuan (also spelled Sichuan) pepper is not a true pepper, but the dried berries of a Chinese shrub. It has a distinctive, fragrant flavour and is used extensively in the Szechuan region in western China, which is noted for its strongly flavoured dishes.

Tamarind paste
This is made from the bitter pods of a large evergreen tree that grows in India. The inner sticky pulp is made into a paste, which is sold in dark brown blocks or in jars. It has an unusual flavour – both tart and sweet at the same time.

Thai fish sauce
Also known as *nam pla*, this is a salty, highly flavoured sauce made from fermented salted fish. It is widely used as a seasoning in Thai cooking. Other similar cuisines, such as Vietnamese, have their own versions, but *nam pla* is most widely available and suitable for all.

Yellow bean sauce
Yellow bean sauce is made from yellow soya beans. It is more of a paste than a sauce, and similar in flavour to soy sauce. It has a pleasant taste and is extremely useful for giving stir-fries an instant Chinese flavour.

chapter 6
Something Special

A collection of distinctive dishes to cook in a wok, plus a menu planner to help you put together fantastic meals for any occasion, from a light lunch to an Oriental buffet.

Chicken and Coconut Milk Soup

Preparation time: 10 minutes
Cooking time: 10 minutes

Serves 4

600 ml (1 pint, 2½ cups) Chicken Stock (see page 154)
6 kaffir lime leaves, torn
1 lemon grass stalk, diagonally sliced
5 cm (2 inch) piece of galangal or fresh root ginger, peeled and
    thinly sliced
250 ml (8 fl oz, 1 cup) Coconut Milk (see page 156)
8 tablespoons Thai fish sauce
2 teaspoons palm sugar or light brown sugar
6 tablespoons lime juice
250 g (8 oz) boneless, skinless chicken, cut into small pieces
4 tablespoons chilli oil or 4 small fresh chillies, deseeded and
    thinly sliced (optional)

1 Heat the stock and stir in the lime leaves, lemon
grass and galangal. As the stock comes to simmering
point, stir in the coconut milk, fish sauce, sugar and lime
juice. Add the chicken pieces and simmer for 5 minutes.

2 Just before serving, add the chilli oil or fresh chillies,
stir again and serve.

wok tip
To make this soup in advance,
follow step 1, then allow the soup
to cool and chill until required.
Reheat and add the chillies just
before serving.

Crispy Lamb with Lettuce

Preparation time: 10 minutes, plus marinating and chilling
Cooking time: about 15 minutes

Serves 4–6

375 g (12 oz) boneless lamb leg steaks or fillet
2 tablespoons soy sauce
1 tablespoon rice wine or dry sherry
2 garlic cloves, thinly sliced
3 tablespoons cornflour
about 300 ml (½ pint, 1¼ cups) groundnut oil, for frying
½ red pepper, cored, deseeded and finely diced, to garnish

TO SERVE:
8–12 Cos or Romaine lettuce leaves
4 spring onions, very finely shredded
plum sauce

1 Cut the lamb across the grain into strips about 5 cm (2 inches) long and 1 cm (½ inch) thick.

2 Stir together the soy sauce, rice wine or sherry and the garlic in a non-metallic dish. Add the lamb and stir to coat, then cover the dish and leave to marinate in the refrigerator for at least 30 minutes.

3 Sift the cornflour over the lamb, then stir to mix it in with the meat and marinade. Put the lamb, uncovered, in the refrigerator for about 30 minutes more.

4 Heat the oil in a wok until very hot, but not smoking. Fry the lamb in about 4 batches for about 3 minutes per batch, until crisp and browned. Lift the pieces of lamb out of the wok with a slotted spoon and set aside to drain on kitchen paper. Put the lamb in a bowl and garnish with red pepper.

5 To serve, arrange the lettuce and spring onions in separate dishes and let each person make their own parcel. The plum sauce should be spooned on to the lettuce, then the lamb and spring onions sprinkled on top and the lettuce wrapped around them.

wok tip
Marinating the lamb gives it more flavour, while chilling it after coating it in cornflour helps to make it crispy, but if you are in a hurry you can dispense with both marinating and chilling.

Crispy Wrapped Prawns

Preparation time: 20 minutes
Cooking time: 10 minutes

Serves 3–4

16 raw tiger prawns, peeled and deveined, with tails
   left intact
75 g (3 oz) minced pork
½ teaspoon sugar
1 tablespoon finely chopped onion
1 garlic clove, finely chopped
2 teaspoons light soy sauce
12 spring roll wrappers
1 egg white, beaten
vegetable oil, for deep-frying
fresh basil or coriander, to garnish (optional)
Hot Sweet Sauce (see page 156), to serve

1 Finely chop 4 of the raw prawns and mix them with the pork, sugar, onion, garlic and soy sauce in a bowl and set aside.

2 Carefully cut open the remaining 12 prawns, making sure you do not cut right through them. Keep the shell-on tails uncut.

3 Put 1 teaspoon or more of the pork mixture on to each opened prawn. Take a spring roll wrapper and pull one corner about three-quarters of the way towards the opposite corner. Place a prawn on to the double thickness of wrapper, leaving the tail free, and roll it up, tucking the ends in and sealing it with a little egg white. Continue until all the prawns are wrapped.

4 Heat the oil in a wok and deep-fry the rolls, in two batches, until golden – this should take about 5 minutes. Remove from the wok and drain on kitchen paper. Garnish with basil or coriander, if using, and serve with hot sweet sauce for dipping.

wok tip
Arrange these mouth-watering wrapped prawns on a platter with other irresistible savouries for an informal supper with friends, or as part of a buffet.

Deep-fried Fish Parcels

Preparation time: 15 minutes
Cooking time: 3 minutes

Serves 4

4 x 125 g (4 oz) sole fillets
pinch of salt
2 tablespoons rice wine or dry sherry
1 tablespoon vegetable oil, plus extra for deep-frying
2 tablespoons shredded spring onion
2 tablespoons shredded fresh root ginger
Spring Onion Tassels (see page 10), to garnish

1 Cut the fish fillets into 2.5 cm (1 inch) squares. Sprinkle with the salt and toss them in the rice wine or sherry.

2 Cut out 4 x 15 cm (6 inch) squares of greaseproof paper and brush them lightly with the oil. Place some pieces of fish on each square of paper and arrange some shredded spring onion and ginger on top.

3 Fold the pieces of paper into envelopes, tucking in the flaps firmly to secure them.

4 Heat the oil in a wok to 180–190°C (350–375°F), or until a cube of bread browns in 30 seconds. Deep-fry the wrapped fish parcels for 3 minutes. Drain and arrange on a warmed serving dish. Garnish with spring onion tassels and serve immediately. Each diner unwraps their own fish parcel with chopsticks.

wok tip
Use another fish in place of the sole if you prefer. Plaice, cod, sea bass and hoki are all good choices.

Hanoi Fried Halibut

Preparation time: 10 minutes, plus marinating
Cooking time: 10 minutes

Serves 4

750 g (1½ lb) halibut, cut into 2.5 cm (1 inch)
    chunks
3 tablespoons Thai fish sauce
1 teaspoon salt
1 teaspoon pepper
vegetable oil, for frying
2.5 cm (1 inch) piece of galangal, peeled and thinly
    sliced
5 cm (2 inch) piece of fresh root ginger, peeled and
    finely chopped
1 teaspoon ground turmeric
handful of fresh dill, chopped
Soy and Vinegar Dipping Sauce (see page 156), to serve

TO GARNISH:
sliced spring onions
Crushed Roasted Peanuts (see page 157)
fresh coriander and basil sprigs

1 Put the halibut into a bowl, add the fish
sauce, salt and pepper and mix well. Cover and
leave to marinate in the refrigerator for 2
hours.

2 Heat about 5 mm (¼ inch) of oil in a wok.
Add the galangal, ginger and turmeric and stir,
then add the chunks of halibut. Mix well and
cook over a moderate heat, stirring
occasionally, for about 5 minutes, or until the
fish is cooked through. Add the dill and mix in
thoroughly.

3 Garnish the halibut with the spring onions,
peanuts, coriander and basil and serve with
the dipping sauce.

wok tip
In Vietnam, this dish is usually
served in individual bowls over rice
noodles.

Singapore Crab

Preparation time: 15 minutes
Cooking time: 10 minutes

Serves 4

2 tablespoons vegetable oil
2.5 cm (1 inch) piece of fresh root ginger, peeled and
    finely chopped
1 garlic clove, finely chopped
1 teaspoon hot chilli powder
6 tablespoons tomato ketchup
2 tablespoons red wine vinegar
1 tablespoon soft brown sugar
150 ml (¼ pint, ⅔ cup) boiling Fish Stock (see page
    154)
1 large cooked crab, chopped into serving pieces, with
    claws and legs cracked open
salt

TO SERVE:
cucumber curls or slices
prawn crackers
boiled rice

1 Heat the oil in a wok over moderate heat.
Add the ginger and garlic and stir-fry for 2–3
minutes, until softened, taking care not to let
them brown.

2 Add the chilli powder and stir well to
combine, then add the ketchup, vinegar and
sugar and bring to the boil. Add the boiling
fish stock, then the pieces of crab. Cook,
stirring constantly, for about 5 minutes, or
until the crab is heated through, then add salt
to taste.

3 Serve hot, with cucumber curls or slices,
prawn crackers and boiled rice handed
separately.

wok tip
When you buy the crab, ask the
fishmonger to remove and discard
the inedible parts of it for you.

Lemon Chicken

Preparation time: 15 minutes
Cooking time: about 20 minutes

Serves 2

1 egg white
2 teaspoons cornflour
pinch of salt
2 boneless, skinless chicken breasts, cut into thin
    strips across the grain
300 ml (½ pint, 1¼ cups) vegetable oil
½ bunch of spring onions, shredded
1 garlic clove, crushed
lemon slices, to garnish

SAUCE:
2 teaspoons cornflour
finely grated rind of ½ lemon
2 tablespoons lemon juice
1 tablespoon soy sauce
2 teaspoons rice wine or dry sherry
2 teaspoons caster sugar

1 First prepare the sauce. Mix the cornflour to a paste with a little water, then stir in the remaining sauce ingredients. Set aside.

2 Lightly beat the egg white in a shallow dish with the cornflour and salt. Add the strips of chicken and turn to coat. Set aside.

3 Heat the oil in a wok until hot, but not smoking. Lift the strips of chicken one at a time out of the egg white mixture with a fork and drop into the hot oil. Shallow-fry, in batches, for about 3–4 minutes, or until golden. Remove with a slotted spoon and drain on kitchen paper. Keep hot.

4 Pour off all but 1 tablespoon of the oil from the wok. Add the spring onions and garlic and stir-fry over a moderate heat for 30 seconds. Stir the sauce, pour into the wok and stir to mix. Increase the heat to high and bring to the boil, stirring constantly.

5 Return the chicken to the wok and stir-fry for 1–2 minutes, or until evenly coated in the sauce. Serve immediately, garnished with lemon slices.

wok tip
This classic dish originated in Hong Kong. Spring onions are included to add crunchiness, but are not essential. If you prefer, you can use green pepper instead, or leave out the vegetables altogether.

Chicken Chop Suey with Garlic

Preparation time: 8 minutes
Cooking time: 8–10 minutes

Serves 4

2 tablespoons vegetable oil
5 spring onions, chopped
2.5 cm (1 inch) piece of fresh root ginger, peeled and chopped
2 garlic cloves, crushed
175 g (6 oz) boneless, skinless chicken breast, cut into thin strips
1 tablespoon tomato purée
2 tablespoons rice wine or dry sherry
2 tablespoons soy sauce
1 teaspoon sugar
8 tablespoons water
300 g (10 oz) bean sprouts
3 eggs, beaten with 2 tablespoons water

1 Heat 1 tablespoon of the oil in a wok, add the spring onions and ginger and stir-fry for 1 minute. Add the garlic and chicken and stir-fry for 2 minutes. Lower the heat, add the tomato purée, rice wine or sherry, soy sauce, sugar and 5 tablespoons of the water. Heat through gently, then transfer to a warmed serving dish.

2 Heat 2 teaspoons of the remaining oil in the wok, add the bean sprouts and the remaining water, and stir-fry for 3 minutes. Add to the serving dish and keep warm.

3 Wipe out the wok and heat the remaining oil. Pour in the beaten eggs and cook until set and crisp. Place on top of the bean sprout mixture and serve immediately.

wok tip
The term chop suey comes from the Chinese word *zasui* which means 'mixed bits'. Leftover cooked meat, fish and vegetables can all be thrown in.

Stir-fried Duck with Mango

wok tip

In this modern recipe, the sweet, juicy fruitiness of mango counteracts the richness of duck meat and tempers the fieriness of red hot chilli. Serve with steamed or boiled rice to make a complete meal.

Preparation time: 15 minutes, plus marinating
Cooking time: about 15 minutes

Serves 2–4

1 large boneless duck breast
1 ripe mango
4 tablespoons groundnut oil
1 large fresh red chilli, deseeded and thinly sliced
4 tablespoons rice wine or dry sherry
75 g (3 oz, ½ cup) Chinese leaves or Savoy cabbage, shredded

MARINADE:
2 tablespoons light or dark soy sauce
1 tablespoon rice wine vinegar or white wine or cider vinegar
½ teaspoon chilli oil
2.5 cm (1 inch) piece of fresh root ginger, peeled and grated
½ teaspoon Chinese five-spice powder

1 Strip the skin and fat off the duck and discard. Cut the duck flesh into thin strips, working diagonally against the grain, then place the strips in a non-metallic dish. Mix together the marinade ingredients, pour into the dish and stir to mix. Cover and leave to marinate at room temperature for about 30 minutes.

2 Meanwhile, cut the mango lengthways into three pieces, avoiding the stone. Peel the pieces of mango and cut the flesh into strips about the same size as the duck.

3 Heat half the oil in a wok. Add half the duck strips and stir-fry over a high heat for 4–5 minutes, or until just tender. Remove the duck with a slotted spoon and repeat with the remaining oil and duck.

4 Return all of the duck to the wok and sprinkle with the chilli and rice wine or sherry. Toss to mix, then add the mango and Chinese leaves or cabbage and toss for 1–2 minutes, until the leaves start to wilt. Serve immediately.

Warm Duck Salad

Preparation time: 8–10 minutes
Cooking time: 3 minutes

Serves 2

¼ cold cooked duck or 1 cooked duck breast
6 small fresh green chillies, deseeded and thinly sliced
½ red onion, thinly sliced
25 g (1 oz, 1 cup) fresh coriander leaves and stalks, finely
  chopped
½ tomato, cut into quarters
4 tablespoons lime juice
1 heaped teaspoon palm sugar or light brown sugar
1½ tablespoons Thai fish sauce

TO SERVE:
lettuce leaves
fresh mint leaves

1 Take the skin and meat off the duck and cut the flesh
into small pieces.

2 Heat a wok until hot, then turn off the heat. Put the
duck into the wok to warm it through, then add all the
remaining ingredients, stirring and turning them
thoroughly for 3 minutes.

3 To serve, arrange the lettuce and mint leaves on the
side of a plate and arrange the duck salad beside them.
Serve immediately.

wok tip
Serve this warm salad as part
of a Thai meal, with a selection of
other dishes with rice and noodles.
Alternatively, it could be eaten as
a starter.

Orange Glazed Pork

Preparation time: 15 minutes
Cooking time: 10 minutes

Serves 3–4

thinly pared rind of 1 large orange, cut into
   matchsticks
3 tablespoons vegetable oil
500 g (1 lb) pork fillet, thinly sliced across the grain
1 onion, finely chopped
2.5 cm (1 inch) piece of fresh root ginger, peeled and
   finely chopped
4 tablespoons orange juice
4 tablespoons clear honey
2 tablespoons crunchy peanut butter
2 tablespoons soy sauce
1/2 teaspoon chilli powder
fresh mint sprigs, to garnish

1 Blanch the strips of orange rind in boiling water for 1 minute. Drain, rinse under cold water and drain again. Set aside.

2 Heat 2 tablespoons of the oil in a wok over moderate heat. Add the pork strips, increase the heat to high and stir-fry for 3–4 minutes, or until lightly coloured on all sides. Tip the pork and its juices into a bowl and set aside.

3 Heat the remaining oil in the wok. Add the onion and ginger and stir-fry for 2–3 minutes, until softened, but not browned. Stir in the orange juice, honey, peanut butter, soy sauce and chilli powder, bring to the boil and stir for 1 minute.

4 Return the pork and its juices to the wok, add half of the orange rind and mix well. Toss until all the ingredients are combined and the pork is piping hot. Serve immediately, sprinkled with the remaining orange rind and mint sprigs.

wok tip
Choose a large, sweet, juicy orange for the best results.

Hot Thai Beef Salad

Preparation time: 15 minutes
Cooking time: 5–10 minutes

Serves 4

2 tablespoons vegetable oil
500 g (1 lb) rump or fillet steak, cut into thin strips across the grain
3 garlic cloves, finely chopped
2 fresh green chillies, thinly sliced
8 tablespoons lemon juice
1 tablespoon Thai fish sauce
2 teaspoons caster sugar
2 ripe papayas, peeled and thinly sliced
½ large cucumber, cut into matchsticks
75 g (3 oz) bean sprouts
1 crisp lettuce, shredded
chilli sauce, to serve (optional)

1 Heat the oil in a wok over a moderate heat. Add the steak, garlic and chillies, increase the heat to high and stir-fry for 3–4 minutes, or until the steak is browned on all sides. Pour in the lemon juice and fish sauce, add the sugar and stir-fry until sizzling.

2 Remove the wok from the heat. Remove the steak from the liquid with a slotted spoon and toss together with the papayas, cucumber, bean sprouts and lettuce. Drizzle the liquid from the wok over the salad ingredients as a dressing and serve hot with a bowl of chilli sauce, if liked.

wok tip
To make Thai Beef Salad with Mango substitute 2 ripe mangoes for the papayas. Serve hot on a bed of fresh coriander instead of lettuce, drizzled with the liquid from the wok.

Fillet of Beef with Sesame Seeds

Preparation time: 15 minutes, plus marinating
Cooking time: 3–6 minutes

Serves 4

4 large garlic cloves, crushed
1½ tablespoons light soy sauce
1 tablespoon Thai fish sauce
1 teaspoon sesame oil
1 tablespoon palm sugar or light brown sugar
1 teaspoon pepper
3 small fresh red chillies, deseeded and finely chopped
2 tablespoons groundnut oil
500 g (1 lb) beef fillet, thinly sliced
2 teaspoons sesame seeds, toasted
Chinese chives, to garnish
boiled or steamed rice, to serve

1 Mix the garlic, soy sauce, fish sauce, sesame oil, sugar, pepper and chillies in a bowl with 1 tablespoon of the groundnut oil. Add the beef slices, mix thoroughly, cover and leave to marinate in the refrigerator overnight.

2 Heat the remaining oil in a wok and, when it is very hot, add the beef slices in one layer. Cook quickly, about 1½ minutes on each side, and remove to a warmed plate. Cover and keep warm while you cook the remaining slices, if you could not fit them all in at once. Sprinkle with the sesame seeds, garnish with chives and serve with rice.

wok tip
Strictly speaking, the fiery heat of chillies is not in the seeds, but in the membranes surrounding them. However, deseeding them removes most of these membranes at the same time.

Tangerine Beef

Preparation time: 15 minutes, plus freezing and marinating
Cooking time: about 15 minutes

Serves 2–3

375 g (12 oz) rump steak, trimmed of all fat
3 tablespoons groundnut oil
4 shallots, cut lengthways into chunks
200 ml (7 fl oz, 1 cup) Beef Stock (see page 154) or water
2 tablespoons soy sauce
2 tablespoons rice wine or dry sherry
3 tangerines, peeled and segmented, with their juice
1 fresh green chilli, deseeded and very finely chopped
1–2 teaspoons sugar
salt and pepper
small handful of fresh coriander leaves, to garnish

MARINADE:
2 pieces dried citrus peel
2 tablespoons soy sauce
1 tablespoon rice wine vinegar or white wine or cider vinegar
1 tablespoon cornflour
1 teaspoon sugar

1 Wrap the beef in clingfilm and place it in the freezer for 1–2 hours, until it is just hard. Meanwhile, soak the citrus peel for the marinade in hot water for about 30 minutes, until softened, then drain and chop finely.

2 Remove the beef from the freezer and unwrap it, then slice it into thin strips, working across the grain. Put the strips in a non-metallic dish. Whisk together all the marinade ingredients, pour the marinade over the beef and stir to mix. Leave to marinate at room temperature for about 30 minutes, or until the beef is completely thawed out.

3 Heat 1 tablespoon of the oil in a wok. Add about half of the beef and stir-fry over a high heat for 3 minutes.

Transfer to a plate with a slotted spoon and repeat with another tablespoon of the oil and the remaining beef.

4 Heat the remaining oil in the wok, then add the shallots, stock or water, soy sauce, rice wine or sherry and the juice from the tangerines. Sprinkle in the chilli, sugar and a little salt and pepper. Bring to the boil, stirring, then cook, stirring constantly, for about 5 minutes until the liquid has reduced.

5 Return the beef to the wok and toss vigorously for 1–2 minutes, until all the ingredients are combined and coated with sauce. Add about two-thirds of the tangerine segments and toss quickly to mix, then taste for seasoning. Serve hot, garnished with the remaining tangerine segments and the coriander.

wok tip
To segment the tangerines, peel the whole fruit, then slice vertically between the membranes to release the segments. Hold the fruit over a bowl to and squeeze the membranes to extract any remaining juice.

Mixed Egg-fried Noodles

Preparation time: 10 minutes
Cooking time: 20 minutes

Serves 4

4 tablespoons groundnut oil
1 garlic clove, crushed
1 shallot or small onion, thinly sliced
125 g (4 oz) fresh egg noodles
grated rind and juice of 1 lime
2 teaspoons soy sauce
125 g (4 oz) boneless, skinless chicken breast or pork loin, sliced
125 g (4 oz) crabmeat or prepared squid
125 g (4 oz) raw prawns, peeled and deveined
1 tablespoon yellow bean sauce
1 tablespoon Thai fish sauce
2 tablespoons palm sugar or light brown sugar
2 eggs
2 fresh red chillies, deseeded and chopped
pepper

TO GARNISH:
fresh coriander leaves
finely sliced lime rind

1 Heat half of the oil in a wok. Add the garlic and shallot or onion and stir-fry quickly until golden and tender.

2 Plunge the egg noodles into boiling water for a few seconds. Drain well and add to the wok. Stir-fry with the grated lime rind, lime juice and soy sauce for 3–4 minutes. Remove, drain and keep warm.

3 Add the remaining oil to the wok together with the chicken or pork, crabmeat or squid and the prawns. Stir-fry over a high heat until cooked. Season with pepper, then stir in the bean paste, fish sauce and sugar.

4 Break the eggs into the wok and stir gently until the mixture sets. Add the chillies and check the seasoning. Mix in the noodles and heat through over a low heat. Serve garnished with coriander leaves and lime rind.

wok tip
Squid is available ready-prepared in most supermarkets and simply needs to be sliced before adding to the wok. Take care not to overcook it, however, or it will become chewy.

Baby Vegetable Stir-fry with Orange and Oyster Sauce

Preparation time: 12 minutes
Cooking time: 12–15 minutes

Serves 4–6

2 tablespoons oil
175 g (6 oz) baby carrots
175 g (6 oz) baby sweetcorn cobs
175 g (6 oz) small button mushrooms
salt and pepper
fresh parsley, to garnish

SAUCE:
2 tablespoons cornflour
4 tablespoons water
finely grated rind and juice of 1 large orange
2 tablespoons oyster sauce
1 tablespoon rice wine or dry sherry

1 To make the sauce, blend the cornflour in a jug with the measured water, then add the orange rind and juice, oyster sauce and rice wine or sherry. Stir well to combine.

2 Heat the oil in a wok. Add the carrots and sweetcorn and stir-fry for 5 minutes, then add the mushrooms and stir-fry for 3–4 minutes.

3 Pour in the sauce mixture and bring to the boil over a high heat, stirring constantly until thickened and glossy. Add salt and pepper to taste, garnish with parsley and serve immediately.

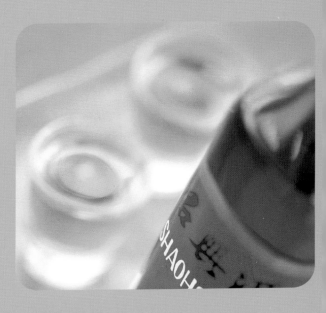

wok tip
This dish is flavoursome enough to make a central dish or main course. Serve with egg noodles or boiled or steamed rice.

Menu planner

These are some suggested menus for different occasions, whether it's a lazy Sunday lunch, or a smart dinner party. It's easy enough to double up quantities for some of the recipes if you have a lot of guests, or reduce them accordingly for smaller parties. The dishes in each menu offer a balanced meal, but by all means swap one or two of the recipes for something else if you are not too keen. If you are entertaining and the pressure is on, ask a friend to bring their wok and come and help as many of the dishes require last-minute cooking.

Light lunch
Vietnamese Dumplings (page 79)
Laksa (page 68)

Thai treats
Chicken and Coconut Milk Soup (page 120)
Crispy Wrapped Prawns (page 122)
Thai Green Chicken Curry (page 61)
Stuffed Thai Omelette (page 27)
White Cabbage Salad (page 92)
Special Egg-fried Rice (page 66)

Lazy Sunday lunch
Wheat Noodle Soup with Marinated Chicken (page 78)
White Cabbage Salad (page 92)

Vietnamese selection
Vietnamese Chicken Rolls (page 20)
Vietnamese Dumplings (page 79)
Hanoi Fried Halibut (page 124)
Paddyfield Pork (page 86)
Mixed Vegetables with Lemon Grass (page 91)
plain boiled rice

Special occasion feast
Crispy Wrapped Prawns (page 122)
Crab Cakes (page 22)
Crispy Lamb with Lettuce (page 121)
Sweet-and-sour Red-cooked Fish (page 80)
Szechuan Scallops (page 59)
Fillet of Beef with Sesame Seeds (page 133)
Pak Choi with Garlic and Oyster Sauce (page 52)
Singapore Noodles (page 70)
Caramelized Bananas (page 142)

Cosy family supper
Lemon Chicken (page 126)
Stir-fried Mixed Vegetables (page 53)
Prawn Vermicelli (page 39)
Caramelized Bananas (page 142)

Oriental buffet
Spring Rolls (page 15)
Fried Wontons (page 16)
Crispy Seaweed (page 17)
Green Peppers Stuffed with Pork and Ginger (page 21)
Spicy Fishcakes (page 103)
Chicken with Chilli and Black Bean Sauce (page 108)
Orange Glazed Pork (page 130-1)
Spring Lamb Stir-fried with Garlic (page 48)
plain boiled rice

Vegetarian feast
Vegetable Pakoras (page 18–19)
Crispy Seaweed (page 17)
Potato and Fenugreek Samosas (pages 24–5)
Baby Vegetable Stir-fry with Orange and Oyster Sauce
    (page 136)
Stir-fried Mushrooms (page 50)
Stir-fried Mixed Vegetables (page 56)
Braised Aubergines (pages 106–7)
Burmese Coconut Rice (page 67)
Egg-fried Noodles with Vegetables and Tofu (page 96)
Toffee Apples Peking Style (page 147)

Traditional Chinese
Spring Rolls (page 15)
Green Peppers Stuffed with Pork and Ginger (page 21)
Quick-fried Fish in Yellow Bean Sauce (pages 36–7)
Cashew Chicken with Garlic, Wine and Ginger (page 42)
Cantonese Pork in Sweet-and-sour Sauce (page 65)
Shanghai Stir-fry (page 72)
Chow Mein (page 69)
Special Egg-fried Rice (page 66)
Red Bean Paste Pancakes (page 145)

Large party
Cellophane Noodle Soup (page 14)
Vietnamese Chicken Rolls (page 20)
Squid and Green Peppers (page 41)
Chicken and Lemon Grass Curry (page 110)
Fried Pork Balls (page 45)
plain boiled rice
Thai Fried Noodles (page 71)
fruit platter

Seafood selection
Potstickers (page 58)
Crab Cakes (page 22)
Deep-fried Fish Parcels (page 123)
Rapid Fried Prawns (page 38)
Scallops with Lemon and Ginger (page 40)
Singapore Crab (page 125)
Prawn Vermicelli (page 39)
Burmese Coconut Rice (page 67)
Fried Apple and Coconut Cakes (page 146)

Chilli-lover's feast
Chicken and Coconut Milk Soup (page 120)
Fried Wontons (page 16)
Burmese Chicken Curry with Cellophane Noodles
    (page 84)
Lamb with Spicy Hot Sauce (page 112)
Spicy Fried Rice with Red Chillies (page 93)
Green Bean Sambal (page 113)

Prepare-ahead meal
Chicken and Coconut Milk Soup (page 120)
Northern Thai Salad (page 28)
exotic fruits

Vegetarian supper
Thai Fried Noodles (page 71)
Mixed Vegetables with Lemon Grass (page 91)
Shanghai Stir-fry (page 72)

chapter 7
Sweet Temptations

Add the finishing touch to your meal
by cooking a dessert in a wok.
The relaxed style of Oriental eating
lends itself to entertaining, so why not
think about giving an Asian-themed
party? There are lots of ideas here
to inspire you.

Fried Apple and Coconut Cakes

Preparation time: 20 minutes, plus standing
Cooking time: 5–10 minutes

Serves 4

125 g (4 oz, ⅔ cup) palm sugar or light brown sugar
400 ml (14 fl oz, 1¾ cups) water
250 g (8 oz, 2 cups) rice flour
1 egg
2 teaspoons baking powder
pinch of salt
150 g (5 oz, 1⅓ cups) freshly grated coconut
4 apples
vegetable oil, for deep-frying
icing sugar, for dusting
crème fraîche or whipped double cream, to serve

1 Put the sugar and measured water in a saucepan and heat gently, stirring constantly, until the sugar has dissolved. Bring to a boil, then stir gently for 2–3 minutes, until syrupy. Remove from the heat and set aside to cool.

2 Combine the rice flour, egg, baking powder, salt and coconut in a large bowl, mixing to a smooth paste.

3 Pour in the cooled syrup and beat to make a smooth batter. Set aside for 20 minutes. Core the apples and cut into rings, then add the rings to the batter.

4 Heat the oil in a wok to 180–190°C (350–375°F), or until a cube of bread browns in 30 seconds. Drop in the apple rings covered in generous amounts of batter and deep-fry, in batches, until golden brown on both sides, turning once. Remove and drain on kitchen paper. Dust with icing sugar and serve hot with crème fraîche or whipped double cream.

wok tip
Chunks of firm banana, mango or pear could be used instead of the apples.

Toffee Apples Peking Style

Preparation time: 15 minutes
Cooking time: 15–20 minutes

Serves 4

125 g (4 oz, 1 cup) plain flour
1 egg
100 ml (3½ fl oz, ½ cup less 2 tablespoons) water
600 ml (1 pint, 2½ cups) sunflower oil
4 crisp apples, peeled, cored and cut into thick slices

SYRUP:
6 tablespoons sugar
1 tablespoon sunflower oil
2 tablespoons water
3 tablespoons golden syrup

1 Mix together the flour, egg and water to make a batter. Heat the oil in a wok to 180–190°C (350–375°F), or until a cube of bread browns in 30 seconds.

2 Dip the apple slices into the batter, then deep-fry for 2 minutes in batches. Remove from the wok and drain on kitchen paper.

3 To make the syrup, heat the sugar in another large pan or wok and add the oil and water. Dissolve the sugar over a gentle heat, then simmer for 5 minutes, stirring constantly. Add the golden syrup and boil the mixture until the syrup forms brittle threads when dropped into iced water.

4 Add the fried apples to the syrup and turn to coat each piece all over. Remove the apple pieces with a slotted spoon and drop into iced water. Quickly remove from the water and serve.

wok tip
These scrumptious apple pieces, encased in crisp, fine, toffee jackets, make a popular dessert served in Chinese restaurants all over the world.

Rice Fritters with Coconut and Vanilla

Preparation time: 10 minutes
Cooking time: about 8–10 minutes

Serves 4–6

165 g (5½ oz, 1¼ cups) medium-grain rice, cooked
2 eggs, beaten
3 tablespoons sugar
½ teaspoon vanilla essence
50 g (2 oz, ½ cup) plain flour
1 tablespoon baking powder
pinch of salt
25 g (1 oz, ⅓ cup) desiccated coconut
vegetable oil, for deep-frying
sifted icing sugar, for sprinkling

1 Put the rice, eggs, sugar and vanilla in a bowl and mix well. Sift together the flour, baking powder and salt, then stir into the rice mixture. Stir in the coconut.

2 Heat the oil in a wok to 180–190°C (350–375°F), or until a cube of bread browns in 30 seconds. Drop tablespoons of the mixture into the hot oil, 1 at a time, and deep-fry until golden on all sides. Drain on kitchen paper.

3 Transfer to a warmed serving dish and sprinkle generously with icing sugar. Serve hot.

wok tip
To make Rice Fritters with Mango, add the finely chopped flesh of ½ a mango to the rice mixture when you add the eggs.

Fried Sweet Potato Balls with Candied Fruits and Sesame Seeds

Preparation time: 10 minutes
Cooking time: 25–30 minutes

Serves 4–6

500 g (1 lb) sweet potatoes
125 g (4 oz, 1 cup) rice flour
50 g (2 oz, ⅓ cup) soft brown sugar
125 g (4 oz, ⅔ cup) crystallized fruit, chopped
50 g (2 oz, ⅓ cup) sesame seeds, lightly toasted
vegetable oil, for deep-frying

1 Cook the sweet potatoes in boiling water for 20 minutes, until tender. Drain and peel. Mash the flesh and gradually beat in the rice flour and sugar. Stir in the crystallized fruit.

2 Roll the mixture into walnut-sized balls with dampened hands, then coat with sesame seeds.

3 Heat the oil in a wok to 180–190°C (350–375°F), or until a cube of bread browns in 30 seconds. Deep-fry the potato balls for 5–7 minutes, until golden brown. Drain on kitchen paper and serve hot.

wok tip
Sweet potatoes can have either white or orange flesh. Orange sweet potatoes are a prettier colour, but either can be used in this dish.

Caramelized Bananas

Preparation time: 15 minutes
Cooking time: 10 minutes

Serves 4

4 bananas
60 g (2½ oz, ½ cup) hazelnuts, toasted and
  finely chopped
25 g (1 oz, ½ cup) fresh breadcrumbs
vegetable oil, for deep-frying

SAUCE:
20 g (¾ oz, 1½ tablespoons) butter
150 g (5 oz, 1 cup) soft brown sugar
4 tablespoons water
300 ml (½ pint, 1¼ cups) Coconut Milk (see
  page 156)

1 Peel the bananas and cut them in half
lengthways, then cut each piece in half again.
Mix together the hazelnuts and breadcrumbs
in a dish and coat the banana pieces well,
pressing the crumbs on to them.

2 Heat all the sauce ingredients in a small,
heavy-based saucepan, stirring constantly, to
make a caramel sauce.

3 Heat the oil in a wok to 180–190°C
(350–375°F), or until a cube of bread browns
in 30 seconds. Deep-fry the bananas, in
batches, for 2 minutes, or until golden brown.
Transfer the bananas to kitchen paper to drain.
To serve, place the bananas on individual
dishes and pour over the warm caramel sauce.

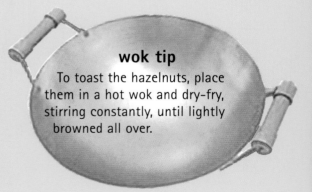

wok tip
To toast the hazelnuts, place
them in a hot wok and dry-fry,
stirring constantly, until lightly
browned all over.

Indonesian Fried Bananas

Preparation time: 10 minutes
Cooking time: 15 minutes

Serves 4–6

150 g (5 oz, 1¼ cups) self-raising flour
1 tablespoon tapioca or plain flour
200 g (7 oz, 1¾ cups) rice flour
1 teaspoon finely grated lime rind
2 teaspoons caster sugar
400 ml (14 fl oz, 1¾ cups) water
oil, for deep-frying
8–10 bananas, sliced lengthways
icing sugar, for dusting

1 Sift the self-raising flour, tapioca and rice flour into a bowl and stir in the grated lime rind and sugar. Gradually add the measured water and beat to a smooth batter.

2 Heat the oil in a wok until a cube of bread browns in 3–4 minutes. Dip the pieces of banana into the batter and then straight into the hot oil. Deep-fry about 6 pieces of banana at a time, turning them once. When the bananas are crisp and golden brown, remove from the wok with a slotted spoon and drain on kitchen paper.

3 To serve, sprinkle with icing sugar and eat while still warm.

wok tip
Known as *Pisang Goreng*, these delicious fritters are best made with firm bananas. You could also use apple wedges or plantains.

Red Bean Paste Pancakes

Preparation time: 10 minutes
Cooking time: about 20 minutes

Serves 8

12 small pancakes
12 tablespoons sweetened red bean paste
about 300 ml (½ pint, 1¼ cups) groundnut oil,
    for deep-frying
caster sugar, for sprinkling

1 Place one pancake on a board or work
surface and spread 1 tablespoon of the red
bean paste in the centre. Brush water all
around the edge of the pancake, then fold the
rounded side nearest to you over the paste.
Fold the two opposite sides into the centre,
then fold the top flap down. Repeat with the
remaining pancakes.

2 Heat the oil in a wok to 180–190°C
(350–375°F), or until a cube of bread browns
in 30 seconds. Deep-fry the pancakes, 1 at a
time, for 1–2 minutes, or until crisp and
golden on both sides, turning them once. Drain
the pancakes on kitchen paper, then cut in
half. Serve warm, sprinkled liberally with
caster sugar.

wok tip
The pancakes used are the
same as the ones served with
Peking duck. You can make these
yourself or buy them ready-made.
If you can't get red bean paste,
sweetened chestnut purée
can be used instead.

Party time!

The easy informality of eating Asian food makes meal times relaxed and pleasurable. Rather than a set pattern of starter, main course and dessert, a selection of various dishes, often including soup, is placed on the table at the same time and everyone helps themselves. Serving all the dishes at once makes Asian food ideal for entertaining, and it can easily be 'stretched' to accommodate an extra guest or two, simply with the addition of more rice or noodles.

Mix and match

While all the different wok cuisines have much in common, each has its own traditions, too. Once you have decided on a party with an Asian theme, you don't have to be truly authentic when it comes to choosing recipes, decorating the table and serving the food and drink. Feel free to mix and match influences to suit you and your guests. You may decide to add a Western touch to an Eastern meal by serving the soup at the beginning of the meal, for example, or to combine Thai flavours with Chinese chopsticks. (An added advantage of a help-your-self-style meal where each guest keeps their own bowl and chopsticks throughout the meal is that there is less washing-up!)

Planning the meal

The fact that all the dishes are served together does not mean that an Asian meal is set out at random. On the contrary, the dishes should be carefully chosen to complement each other and to achieve the ideals of balance and harmony. Contrasts of taste (sweet, sour,

salty, bitter, piquant), colour, appearance and texture are very important.

When catering for a crowd, increasing the number of dishes on offer rather than the quantity of ingredients will provide more variety on the table. Since stir-fry dishes need constant attention and should be served as soon as they are ready, cooking for your party will be easier if you choose just a couple of stir-fries and combine them with dishes that can be prepared to some extent in advance, for example, steamed, braised, roasted or cold dishes. For balance, include dishes with fish, poultry, tofu and pork or beef. Supplement these with carefully chosen vegetable, rice and noodle dishes. (See pages 138–9 for menu suggestions.)

Desserts as they are known in the West are rare in Asian meals — usually only for very special occasions. Fresh tropical fruit like lychees and mangoes are the more usual end to a meal.

Drinks

Lager is a popular choice to serve with Asian food and many brands of Asian beer are now readily available outside their country of origin. If you want to serve wine with the meal, choose light, fruity wines in both red and white varieties or, serve a Chinese wine if you can find one but be aware that most are grain- rather than grape-based and have a high alcohol content!

If you prefer, serve tea with the food — jasmine tea is always popular. Make a pot and serve the tea in small cups without sugar or milk. With Chinese food, however, it is more usual to serve tea only at the end of the meal to aid digestion.

How to use chopsticks

1 Take one chopstick — preferably wooden or bamboo, as plastic tend to slip — and place it in the hollow between thumb and index finger; rest its lower end between the tips of the third and fourth fingers. This chopstick will remain stationary at all times.

2 Hold the other chopstick between the tips of the index and middle fingers and use the tip of the thumb to keep it in place.

3 Keeping the lower chopstick still, use your index finger to move the upper chopstick towards the lower one until their tips are close together and you can pick up a piece of food.

4 It takes practice to master using chopsticks but if you cannot get the hang of it use a fork or spoon instead to avoid going hungry!

Setting the scene

It's fairly easy to set the scene for an Asian-style meal and you will gain loads of fun ideas if you visit an Oriental store. You can buy inexpensive paper banners, fans, scented candles, incense sticks and paper lanterns to decorate the room, as well as small items for the table such as Chinese paper dragons, paper umbrellas or little Buddhas. You could even make your own origami figures to decorate place settings.

Have a bowl of water with floating candles and exotic flower heads as the table centrepiece and arrange block candles in holders of plain glass or with Oriental motifs along the table. Lay place settings with mats made of hessian, raffia or bamboo and sprinkle the tablecloth with star anise, cinnamon sticks, lemon grass, sprigs of coriander or lime leaves for decoration. Use Oriental-style tableware if possible and set chopsticks beside each plate or bowl, paired together with narrow ribbon or raffia. Wrap individual fortune cookies in cellophane, secure

each one with raffia and attach to a name tag decorated with Chinese motifs and bearing a guest's name to denote where everyone should sit.

You and your guests could even dress up in Oriental-style clothes – silky pyjamas and kimonos or other suitable garments in Thai silk or shiny fabrics with bold patterns. Ladies could wear silk flowers in their hair or could decoratively arrange chopsticks in their hair.

chapter 8
Back to Basics

Essential stocks and sauces, curry pastes,
flavourings and garnishes to make
all the dishes you cook in your wok
both authentic and delicious.

Fish Stock

Preparation time: 10 minutes
Cooking time: 20 minutes

Makes about 1.8 litres (3 pints, 7½ cups)

1.5 kg (3 lb) non-oily fish trimmings
1 onion, roughly chopped
white part of 1 small leek, chopped
1 celery stick, roughly chopped
1 bay leaf
6 parsley stalks
10 black peppercorns
475 ml (16 fl oz, 2 cups) dry white wine
1.8 litres (3 pints, 7½ cups) cold water

1 Place all the ingredients in a large saucepan. Gradually bring to the boil, then immediately reduce the heat to a slow simmer.

2 Simmer for 20 minutes, skimming off any scum from the surface. Strain the stock through a muslin-lined sieve and leave to cool before chilling in the refrigerator.

Chicken Stock

Preparation time: 5–10 minutes
Cooking time: about 2½ hours

Makes 1 litre (1¾ pints, 4½ cups)

1 cooked chicken carcass, roughly chopped
raw chicken giblets and trimmings
1 onion, roughly chopped
2 large carrots, roughly chopped
1 celery stick, roughly chopped
1 bay leaf
a few parsley stalks
1 thyme sprig
1.8 litres (3 pints, 7¼ cups) cold water

1 Place all the ingredients in a large saucepan and bring to the boil. Skim off any scum from the surface.

2 Lower the heat and simmer for 2–2½ hours. Strain the stock through a muslin-lined sieve and leave to cool before chilling in the refrigerator.

Beef Stock

Preparation time: 15 minutes
Cooking time: about 4½ hours

Makes about 1.5 litres (2½ pints, 6½ cups)

750 g (1½ lb) shin of beef, cubed
2 onions, roughly chopped
2–3 carrots, roughly chopped
2 celery sticks, roughly chopped
1 bay leaf
1 bouquet garni
6 black peppercorns
1.8 litres (3 pints, 7½ cups) water
½ teaspoon salt

1 Boil all the ingredients in a large saucepan, then immediately reduce the heat to a slow simmer.

2 Cover and simmer for 4 hours, skimming off any scum from the surface. Strain the stock through a muslin-lined sieve and leave to cool before chilling in the refrigerator.

Vegetable Stock

Preparation time: 10 minutes
Cooking time: about 45 minutes

Makes about 1 litre (1¾ pints, 4½ cups)

500 g (1 lb) chopped mixed vegetables (carrots, leeks, celery, onion, mushrooms)
1 garlic clove
6 black peppercorns
2 parsley sprigs
2 thyme sprigs
1 bay leaf
1.2 litres (2 pints, 5 cups) water

1 Place all the ingredients in a large saucepan. Gradually bring to the boil, then immediately reduce the heat to a slow simmer.

2 Simmer for 30 minutes, skimming off any scum from the surface. Strain the stock through a muslin-lined sieve and leave to cool before chilling in the refrigerator.

Red Curry Paste

Preparation time: 15 minutes

10 large fresh red chillies, stalks removed
2 teaspoons coriander seeds
5 cm (2 inch) piece of galangal or fresh root ginger, peeled and
   finely chopped
1 lemon grass stalk, finely chopped
4 garlic cloves, halved
1 shallot, roughly chopped
1 teaspoon lime juice
2 tablespoons groundnut oil

1 Put all the ingredients in a blender or food processor and blend to a thick paste. Alternatively, pound all the ingredients together in a mortar with a pestle.

2 Transfer the paste to an airtight container and store in the refrigerator for up to 3 weeks.

Green Curry Paste

Preparation time: 15 minutes

15 small fresh green chillies
4 garlic cloves, halved
2 lemon grass stalks, finely chopped
2 kaffir lime leaves, torn
2 shallots, roughly chopped
50 g (2 oz, 1 cup) fresh coriander leaves, stalks and roots
2.5 cm (1 inch) piece of galangal or fresh root ginger, peeled and
   finely chopped
2 teaspoons coriander seeds
1 teaspoon black peppercorns

1 teaspoon peeled lime rind
$\frac{1}{2}$ teaspoon salt
2 tablespoons groundnut oil

1 Put all the ingredients in a blender or food processor and blend to a thick paste. Alternatively, pound all the ingredients together in a mortar with a pestle.

2 Transfer the paste to an airtight container and store in the refrigerator for up to 3 weeks.

Yellow Curry Paste

Preparation time: 15 minutes

2.5 cm (1 inch) piece of galangal or fresh root ginger, peeled and
   finely chopped
1 lemon grass stalk, finely chopped
2 shallots, roughly chopped
3 garlic cloves, halved
2 teaspoons ground turmeric
1 teaspoon ground coriander
1 teaspoon ground cumin
1 teaspoon shrimp paste
$\frac{1}{2}$ teaspoon chilli powder

1 Put all the ingredients in a blender or food processor and blend to a thick paste. Alternatively, pound all the ingredients together in a mortar with a pestle.

2 Transfer the paste to an airtight container and store in the refrigerator for up to 3 weeks.

Garlic Mixture

Preparation time: 5 minutes

2 tablespoons crushed garlic
2 tablespoons chopped fresh coriander stems
$\frac{1}{2}$ teaspoon pepper

1 Put all the ingredients in a mortar and crush with a pestle to form a thick paste.

Coconut Milk and Cream

Preparation time: 5 minutes
Cooking time: about 15 minutes

400 g (14 oz) grated or desiccated coconut
900 ml (1½ pints, 3¾ cups) milk

1 Place the coconut and milk in a saucepan and bring to the boil. Reduce the heat and simmer, stirring occasionally, until the mixture is reduced by one-third.

2 Strain, extracting as much liquid as possible. Pour the strained milk into a bowl and chill in the refrigerator.

3 When it is cold, skim off the thicker 'cream' from the surface. The remaining liquid is coconut milk.

Tamarind Water

Preparation time: 10 minutes
Cooking time: 5 minutes

1 tablespoon tamarind paste
4 tablespoons water

1 Put the tamarind paste and water in a small pan and mix well to dilute the paste. Bring the water to simmering point, then remove from the heat and leave to cool. Strain through a fine sieve, pressing through as much of the paste as possible to give a thick liquid.

Soy and Vinegar Dipping Sauce

Preparation time: 2 minutes

3 tablespoons distilled white vinegar or rice wine vinegar
3 tablespoons dark soy sauce
1½ teaspoons caster sugar
2 small fresh red chillies, thinly sliced

1 Combine all the ingredients in a bowl and stir until the sugar has dissolved.

Chilli Sauce

Preparation time: 3–4 minutes
Cooking time: 10–15 minutes

8 red fresh chillies, chopped
4 garlic cloves, crushed
1 tablespoon Thai fish sauce
2 teaspoons sugar
2 tablespoons lime or lemon juice
½ teaspoon salt
125 ml (4 fl oz, ½ cup) water
2 tablespoons peanut oil

1 Put the chillies, garlic, fish sauce, sugar, lime or lemon juice and the salt in a small saucepan. Stir in the measured water and oil. Bring to a boil, reduce the heat, and simmer gently for 10–15 minutes. Process in a food processor or blender until smooth. Store in an airtight jar in the refrigerator for up to 2 weeks.

Hot Sweet Sauce

Preparation time: 1 minute
Cooking time: 1–2 minutes

125 ml (4 fl oz, ½ cup) distilled white vinegar or rice wine vinegar
75 g (3 oz, ½ cup) palm sugar or light brown sugar
½ teaspoon salt
1 small fresh green chilli, finely chopped
1 small fresh red chilli, finely chopped

1 Pour the vinegar into a small saucepan and place over a gentle heat. Add the sugar and salt and cook, stirring, until the sugar has dissolved. Remove from the heat and allow to cool.

2 Pour the cooled sauce into a small bowl and add the chopped chillies.

Crispy Fried Shallots

Preparation time: 5 minutes
Cooking time: 5 minutes

about 750 ml (1¼ pints, 3 cups) groundnut oil, for deep-frying
25 g (1 oz, ¼ cup) shallots, finely chopped

1 Heat the oil in a wok until it is very hot, but not smoking. Add the shallots and stir for about 1½–2 minutes, until they sizzle and turn golden.

2 Remove from the oil with a slotted spoon, draining off as much oil as possible, and spread them out to dry on kitchen paper. When the shallots are dried and crispy, store in an airtight container for up to 1 month. Cool and reuse the oil.

Crispy Fried Garlic

Preparation time: 5 minutes
Cooking time: 5 minutes

about 750 ml (1¼ pints, 3 cups) groundnut oil, for deep-frying
25 g (1 oz) garlic, thinly sliced

1 Heat the oil in a wok until it is very hot, but not smoking. Add the garlic and stir for about 40 seconds, until it sizzles and turns golden.

2 Remove from the oil with a slotted spoon, draining off as much oil as possible, and spread it out to dry on kitchen paper. When the garlic is dried and crispy, store it in an airtight container for up to 1 month. Cool and reuse the oil.

Crushed Roasted Peanuts

Preparation time: 5 minutes
Cooking time: 5 minutes

25 g (1 oz, ¼ cup) unroasted peanuts

1 Heat a wok and dry-fry the nuts. Stir constantly until the turn a golden colour. Remove from the heat and allow to cool.

2 Place the nuts in a plastic bag and break into small pieces using a rolling pin. Store in an airtight container in the refrigerator for up to 1 month.

Wonton Wrappers

Preparation time: 20 minutes

Makes 18

50 g (2 oz, ½ cup) plain flour
50 g (2 oz, ½ cup) cornflour
2 teaspoons baking powder
pinch of salt
1 egg, lightly beaten
2 tablespoons water

1 Sift the flour, cornflour, baking powder and salt into a bowl and make a well in the centre. Add the egg and measured water and mix to form a stiff dough.

2 Turn out on to a lightly floured surface and knead thoroughly until very smooth. Work quickly so that the dough does not stick to the work surface and avoid dusting with lots of flour. Divide the dough in half and keep one portion covered with clingfilm while you work with the other.

3 Roll out the first portion on a well-floured surface until it is very thin. It should form a square about 25 cm (10 inches) across. The thinner the dough becomes, the better the results, but take care not to rip it as it is very difficult to patch any holes.

4 Trim the edges and cut the dough into 9 small squares. Roll out each of these until very thin and about 10 cm (4 inches) square. Wrap the wonton wrappers in clingfilm to prevent them from drying out and repeat the process with the other portion of dough.

Index

A

apples
  fried apple and coconut cake 142
  toffee apples Peking style 143
artichokes with red peppers 30
aubergines
  braised 106
  and stir-fried pork 87

B

baby vegetables
  stir-fried with orange and oyster sauce 136
  sweetcorn 74
bamboo shoots 74
bananas
  caramelized 146
  Indonesian fried 148
bang bang chicken 64
bean sprouts 74
beef
  fillet with sesame seeds 133
  hot Thai beef salad 132
  mangetout and beef stir-fry 46
  in oyster sauce 90
  stock 154
  tangerine beef 134
black beans
  fermented 116
  sauce 81, 116
black fungus, dried 116
boiling method 9
braised aubergines 106
broccoli, prawns with 23
Burmese
  chicken curry with cellophane noodles 84
  coconut rice 67

C

cake, fried apple and coconut 142
Cantonese pork in sweet-and-sour sauce 65
caramel sauce 146
caramelized bananas 146
cashew chicken with garlic, wine and ginger 42
cellophane noodles
  Burmese chicken curry with 84
  soup 14

chicken
  and aubergine stir-fry 87
  bang bang 64
  Burmese chicken curry with cellophane noodles 84
  cashew chicken with garlic, wine and ginger 42
  with chilli and black bean sauce 108
  chop suey with garlic 127
  and coconut milk soup 120
  ginger chicken with honey 43
  Goan chicken shakuti 109
  green Thai curry 61
  Kashmiri 62
  laksa 68
  lemon 126
  and lemon grass curry 110
  Malaysian orange 60
  with noodles and prawns 97
  sesame stir-fried 44
  and shiitake mushrooms stir-fry 83
  spicy chicken satay 26
  stock 154
  velveting 108
  vermicelli 39
  Vietnamese chicken rolls 20
  wheat noodle soup with marinated chicken 78
chillies 74, 139
  chicken with chilli and black bean sauce 108
  chilli bean paste 116
  chilli flowers 11
  chilli oil 116
  chilli sauce 116, 156
  dried 116
  spicy fried rice with red 93
chinese leaves 74
chop suey, chicken with garlic 127
chopsticks 151
chow mein 69
citrus peel, dried 116
cloud ear fungus 116
coconut, toasted 109
coconut milk and cream 74, 156
coconut rice 67
coriander 74
  relish 18
crab
  cakes 22
  Singapore 125

crispy
  fried garlic 157
  fried shallots 157
  lamb with lettuce 121
  rice with dipping sauce 31
  seaweed 17
  wrapped prawns 122
crushed roasted peanuts 157
cucumber slices 11
curries
  Burmese chicken with cellophane noodles 84
  chicken and lemon grass 110
  king prawn and coconut 105
  new potato 94
  prawns and lemon grass 110
  red curry duck 111
  Sayur Kari 114–15
  Thai green chicken 61
curry pastes 155

D

dark soy sauce 116
deep-fried fish parcels 123
deep-frying method 9, 17
dipping sauces 31, 156
dried black fungus 116
drinks 150
duck
  with mango stir-fry 128
  with pineapple 88
  red curry 111
  stir-fried with shiitake mushrooms 83
  Thai green curry 61
  warm duck salad 129
dumplings
  dumpling pastries 75
  potstickers 58
  Vietnamese 79

E

egg-fried noodles
  mixed with squid 135
  with vegetables and tofu 96
egg-fried rice, special 66

F

fenugreek and potato samosas 24
fish

with black bean sauce 81
deep-fried parcels 123
Hanoi fried halibut 124
low-fat cooking 55
monkfish 36
quick-fried in yellow bean sauce 36–7
scallops with lemon and ginger 40
sole with herbs and satay sauce 102
spicy fishcakes 103
squid and green peppers 41
stock 154
sweet-and-sour red-cooked fish 80
in tamarind sauce 104
see also prawns
fish sauce, Thai 116
five-spice powder 65, 116
fried
  apple and coconut cakes 142
  pork balls 45
  sweet potato balls with candied fruits and sesame seeds 145
  Thai noodles 71
  wontons 16
fritters
  banana 148
  rice with coconut and vanilla 144

G

galangal 74
garlic 74
  crispy fried 157
  mixture 155
garnishes 10–11
ginger 74
  ginger chicken with honey 43
Goan chicken shakuti 109
green bean sambal 113
green curry paste 155
green peppers
  squid and 41
  stuffed with pork and ginger 21

H

Hanoi fried halibut 124
hazelnuts, toasted 146
hoisin sauce 116

hot sweet sauce 156
hot Thai beef salad 132

I

Indonesian fried bananas 148

K

kaffir lime leaves 74–5
Kashmiri chicken 62
king prawn and coconut curry 105

L

laksa 68
lamb
    crispy with lettuce 121
    with spicy hot sauce 112
    spring lamb stir-fried with garlic
        48
laos powder 74
lemon
    chicken 126
    sauce 126
    scallops with lemon and ginger
        40
    slices 11
lemon grass 75
    and chicken curry 110
    mixed vegetables with 91
light soy sauce 116–17
lime leaves, kaffir 74–5
liver, stir-fried with spinach and
        ginger 49
low-fat wok-ing 54–5

M

Malaysian orange chicken 60
mangetout and beef stir-fry 46
mangoes 128, 132, 144
marinades 116–17, 128, 134
meat, low-fat cooking 55
menu planner 138–9
miso paste 98–9
mixed egg-fried noodles 135
mixed vegetables
    with lemon grass 91
    scallop and prawn stir-fry 82
    stir-fried 53, 82
monkfish 36
mushrooms, shiitake 50, 83, 116

N

nam pla (Thai fish sauce) 116
new potato curry 94

noodles 75
    cellophane 14, 84
    with chicken and prawns 97
    low-fat cooking 54
    mixed egg-fried 135
    Singapore 70
    Thai fried 71
    wheat noodle soup with
        marinated chicken 78
Northern Thai salad 28
nuts 4, 99
    cashew chicken with garlic, wine
        and ginger 42
    roasted peanuts 26, 78, 157
    toasted hazelnuts 146

O

oil 10, 54, 60
omelettes
    strips 93
    stuffed 27
orange
    glazed pork 130
    Malaysian chicken 60
    and oyster sauce 136
    sauce 60
oyster sauce 117

P

paddyfield pork 86
pak choi 75
    with garlic and oyster sauce 52
pakoras, vegetable 18
palm sugar 117
pancakes, red bean paste 149
papaya (pawpaw) 75, 132
party planning 150–1
pastes 98–9, 105, 116, 117, 149,
        155
peanuts, roasted 26, 78, 157
peas 99
peppercorns, Szechuan 117
peppers, artichokes with red 30
pineapple, duck with 88
plum sauce 117, 121
pork
    Cantonese in sweet-and-sour
        sauce 65
    fried pork balls 45
    green peppers stuffed with pork
        and ginger 21
    orange glazed 130
    paddyfield 86
    stir-fried with aubergine 87
potatoes
    and fenugreek samosas 24

fried sweet potato balls with
        candied fruits and sesame
        seeds 145
    new potato curry 94
potstickers 58
prawns
    with broccoli 23
    crispy wrapped tiger 122
    king prawn and coconut curry
        105
    and lemon grass curry 110
    noodles with chicken and 97
    prawn vermicelli 39
    rapid fried 38
    and scallop stir-fry with mixed
        vegetables 82

Q

quick-fried fish in yellow bean
        sauce 36–7

R

radish roses 11
rapid fried prawns 38
red bean paste 117
    pancakes 149
red braising method 9, 55
red curry
    duck 111
    paste 155
red peppers, artichokes with 30
red-cooked fish, sweet-and-sour 80
rice 10, 31
    Burmese coconut rice 67
    crispy with dipping sauce 31
    fritters with coconut and vanilla
        144
    low-fat cooking 54
    special egg-fried 66
    spicy fried with red chillies 93
    wine 117
    wine vinegar 117

S

salads
    hot Thai beef 132
    Northern Thai 28
    warm duck 129
    white cabbage 92
sambal, green bean 113
samosas, potato and fenugreek 24
satay, spicy chicken satay 26
satay sauce 26, 102
sauces
    black bean 81

caramel 146
    chilli 156
    dipping 31, 156
    hoisin 116
    hot sweet 156
    lemon 126
    orange 60, 136
    orange and oyster 136
    satay 26, 102
    shoyu 99
    soy 99, 116–17, 156
    spicy hot 112
    sweet-and-sour 38
Sayur Kari 114–15
scallops
    with lemon and ginger 40
    and prawn stir-fry with mixed
        vegetables 82
    Szechuan 59
seaweed, crispy 17
seeds 99
seitan 99
sesame chicken, stir-fried 44
sesame seeds
    paste 117
    seasoning 67
    toasted 64
shakuti chicken 109
shallots, crispy fried 157
Shanghai stir-fry 72–3
shiitake mushrooms 50, 83, 116
shoyu sauce 99
shrimp paste 117
Singapore
    crab 125
    noodles 70
sole with herbs and satay sauce 102
soups
    cellophane noodle 14
    chicken and coconut milk 120
    wheat noodle with marinated
        chicken 78
soy sauce 99, 116–17, 156
soy and vinegar dipping sauce 156
soya 98
special egg-fried rice 66
spice paste 105
spicy
    chicken satay 26
    fishcakes 103
    fried rice with red chillies 93
spinach, stir-fried liver with ginger
        49
spring lamb stir-fried with garlic 48
spring onion tassels 11
spring rolls 15
    wrappers 75
squid

and green peppers 41
mixed egg-fried noodles 135
steaming method 9, 54–5
stir-braising method 9
stir-fries
    baby vegetables with orange and
        oyster sauce 136
    chicken with shiitake mushrooms
        83
    duck with mango 128
    liver with spinach and ginger 49
    mangetout and beef 46
    mixed vegetables 53
    mushrooms 50–1
    pork with aubergine 87
    sesame chicken 44
    Shanghai 72–3
    spring lamb with garlic 48
stir-frying method 9, 32–3
stocks 154–5
stuffed Thai omelette 27
sweet potatoes, fried with candied
    fruits and sesame seeds 145
sweet-and-sour
    red-cooked fish 80
    sauce 38
sweetcorn, baby cobs 74
Szechuan
    peppercorns 117
    scallops 59

T
tamari sauce 99
tamarind
    paste 117
    sauce 104
    water 156
tangerine beef 134
tempeh 98
textured vegetable protein (TVP) 98
Thai
    fish sauce 116, 117
    fried noodles 71
    green chicken curry 61
    Northern Thai salad 28
    stuffed omelette 27
tiger prawns, crispy wrapped 122
toasted
    coconut 109
    hazelnuts 146
    sesame seeds 64
toffee apples Peking style 143
tofu 75, 98, 114
    egg-fried noodles with vegetables
        and 96
    Sayur Kari 114–15
tomatoes
    skinning 27
    tomato roses 11
TVP (textured vegetable protein) 98

V
vegetable pakoras 18
vegetable stock 154
vegetables
    baby vegetables stir-fry with
        orange and oyster sauce 136
    egg-fried noodles and tofu 96
    low-fat cooking 55
    stir-fried mixed 53
    vegetable curry 114
vegetarian
    chow mein 69
    cooking 5, 98–9
velveting chicken 108
vermicelli 39
Vietnamese dishes
    chicken rolls 20
    dumplings 79
    Hanoi fried halibut 124
    mixed vegetables with lemon
        grass 91
    paddyfield pork 86
vinegar, rice wine 117

W
warm duck salad 129
water chestnuts 75, 99
wheat meat (seitan) 99
wheat noodle soup with marinated

chicken 78
white cabbage salad 92
woks 6–9
wontons
    fried 16
    wrappers 16, 75, 157
wood ear fungus 116

Y
yellow bean sauce 117
yellow curry paste 155

Acknowledgements

Executive Editor: Nicola Hill
Editor: Rachel Lawrence
Executive Art Editor: Leigh Jones
Designer: Jo Tapper
Senior Production Controller: Jo Sim
Picture Researcher: Jennifer Veall
Special Photography: David Jordan
Food stylist: Mari Mererid Williams

Photographic Acknowledgements

All photography by David Jordan except for the following:
Octopus Publishing Group Limited/Jean Cazals 42, 65, 69, 102, 127, 141, 145 /Graham Kirk 109/ Sandra Lane 39/David Loftus 68, 70, 78/Neil Mersh 15, 16, 26, 97, 101, 103, 111, 119, 122, 142/Peter Myers 31, 57, 61, 81, 92, 104, 105, 120, 132, 153/ Sean Myers 20/Peter Pugh-Cook 130/ William Reavell 41, 94, 150/Roger Stowell 4 bottom centre left, 12, 21/ Ian Wallace 4 bottom right, 5 bottom centre left, 5 bottom centre right, 13, 14 left, 18, 22, 58, 62, 76, 77, 80, 83 right, 86, 88, 91, 95, 108, 110, 118, 121, 124, 125, 128, 133, 134, 136 centre top, 151, 152/Philip Webb 17/Paul Williams 48
Leigh Jones 27, 129